Jack C. Richards' 50 Tips for Teacher Development

Cambridge Handbooks for Language Teachers

This series, now with over 50 titles, offers practical ideas, techniques and activities for the teaching of English and other languages, providing inspiration for both teachers and trainers.

The Pocket Editions come in a handy, pocket-sized format and are crammed full of tips and ideas from experienced English language teaching professionals, to enrich your teaching practice.

Recent titles in this series:

Recent Pocket Editions:

Jack C. Richards' 50 Tips for Teacher Development

Jack C. Richards

Consultant and editor: Scott Thornbury

CAMBRIDGE
UNIVERSITY PRESS

CAMBRIDGE
UNIVERSITY PRESS

University Printing House, Cambridge CB2 8BS, United Kingdom

One Liberty Plaza, 20th Floor, New York, NY 10006, USA

477 Williamstown Road, Port Melbourne, VIC 3207, Australia

314-321, 3rd Floor, Plot 3, Splendor Forum, Jasola District Centre, New Delhi - 110025, India

79 Anson Road, #06-04/06, Singapore 079906

Cambridge University Press is part of the University of Cambridge.

It furthers the University's mission by disseminating knowledge in the pursuit of
education, learning and research at the highest international levels of excellence.

www.cambridge.org
Information on this title: www.cambridge.org/9781108408363

First published 2017

20 19 18 17 16 15 14 13 12 11 10 9 8 7 6 5 4 3 2 1

A catalogue record for this publication is available from the British Library

ISBN   978-1-108-40836-3   Paperback
ISBN   978-1-108-40837-0   Apple iBook
ISBN   978-1-108-40838-7   Google ebook
ISBN   978-1-108-40839-4   Kindle ebook
ISBN   978-1-108-40840-0   eBooks.com ebook

Contents

Acknowledgements

The authors and publishers acknowledge the following sources of copyright material and are grateful for the permissions granted. While every effort has been made, it has not always been possible to identify the sources of all the material used, or to trace all copyright holders. If any omissions are brought to our notice, we will be happy to include the appropriate acknowledgements on reprinting and in the next update to the digital edition, as applicable.

Text

Cambridge University Press for the text on pp. 18–19 adapted from *Professional Development for Teacher Learning* by Jack C. Richards and Thomas S. C. Farrell. Copyright © 2005 Cambridge University Press. Reproduced with kind permission; Cambridge University Press for the text on pp. 40–41 from *Reflective Teaching in Second Language Classrooms* by Jack C. Richards and Charles Lockhart. Copyright © 1994 Cambridge University Press. Reproduced with kind permission; John Benjamins Publishing Co. for the text on pp. 40–41 from "The use of lesson transcripts for developing teachers' classroom language" by R. Cullen in *Language in Language Teacher Education* edited by Hugh Tappes-Lomax and Gibson Ferguson. Copyright © John Benjamins Publishing Co. Reproduced with kind permission; Pan Macmillan for the text on pp. 47–48 from *Nowhere Man* by Aleksander Hemon. Copyright © 2002 Pan Macmillan. Reproduced with kind permission of Pan Macmillan via PLSclear; Lulu.com for the text on pp. 52–53 from *Trainer Development* by Tony Wright and Rod Bolitho. Copyright © 2007 Tony Wright and Rod Bolitho. Reproduced with kind permission of Tony Wright; Cambridge University Press for the text on pp. 65–66 from *Reflective Teaching in Second Language Classrooms* by Jack C. Richards and Charles Lockhart. Copyright © 1994 Cambridge University Press. Reproduced with kind permission; Jose Lema for the text on pp. 63–64 from an unpublished e-mail. Copyright © Jose Lema. Reproduced with kind permission; Phil Wade, Rob Haines, and Dennis Newson for the text on p. 75 from 'ELT Dogme', https://groups.yahoo.com/neo/groups/dogme/info. Copyright © Phil Wade, Rob Haines, and Dennis Newson; Cambridge University Press for the text on pp. 78–79 from *Motivational Strategies in the Language Classroom* by Zoltán Dörnyei. Copyright © 2001 Cambridge University Press. Reproduced with kind permission; Sara Cotterall for the text on pp. 83–84 from 'Teacher insight provided' by Sara Cotterall. Copyright © Sara Cotterall. Reproduced with kind permission; Cambridge University Press for the text on pp. 87–88 from *Key Issues in Language Teaching* by Jack C. Richards. Copyright © 2015 Cambridge University Press. Reproduced with kind permission; Fiona Mauchline, Jane Arnold, and Rob Haines for the text on p. 102 from 'ELT Dogme', https://groups.yahoo.com/neo/groups/dogme/info. Copyright © Fiona Mauchline, Jane Arnold, and Rob Haines.

The publisher has used its best endeavours to ensure that the URLs for external websites referred to in this book are correct and active at the time of going to press. However, the publisher has no responsibility for the websites and can make no guarantee that a site will remain live or that the content is or will remain appropriate.

Why I wrote this book

I have written this book for language teachers, co-ordinators and others who are interested in pursuing or developing plans for professional development. It includes accounts of strategies that you can use as an individual teacher or with a group of teachers, focusing on different aspects of professional development. Each tip refers to an activity that can facilitate some aspect of teacher development. The purpose of each tip is described, its rationale, and procedures for carrying out the activity.

Why this book: The language teaching profession involves teachers who are at different stages in their professional development. The field of language teaching is also very dynamic and teachers often tell me how difficult it is for them to keep up with changes. As a result, we all need regular opportunities to update our professional knowledge and skills. This is where professional development can play an important role.

The need for ongoing teacher education has been a recurring theme in language teaching circles in recent years, and at conferences and workshops we hear more and more about the importance of teacher-led initiatives such as action research, reflective teaching and team teaching. Opportunities for professional development are crucial for the long-term development of teachers, as well as for the long-term success of the schools and institutions in which we work. However, the need for ongoing renewal of professional knowledge and skills does not suggest that teachers are poorly trained, but simply reflects the fact that not everything teachers need to know can be provided at pre-service level, as well as the fact that the knowledge base of language teaching regularly changes. At the same time, teacher development is a process that takes place over time rather than an event that begins and ends with formal training or graduate education.

The kinds of activities I have included in this book often depend for their success on the active cooperation of program coordinators and others within the school or institution. However, many can also be carried out through the teacher's own individual efforts. I have included tips for both kinds of approaches in this book.

The tips in this book contain a wide variety of activities that you can use to plan and manage aspects of your own professional development. They draw on my many years of experience in working with teachers at different stages in their professional development. The tips address core aspects of teacher development, including such issues as assessing needs and goals, researching teaching and learning, extending knowledge and skills, and expanding professional knowledge.

I believe that the tips presented here will be of interest both to classroom teachers and others in a school who are involved in providing support for teacher development. They are intended to provide ideas for practicing teachers, particularly those who are relatively new to language teaching, as well as experienced teachers, supervisors and others who are interested in promoting a culture of professional development in their schools or institutions. Each tip is described in a straightforward and non-technical way: the goals of each activity are discussed; the methodology or procedures involved in implementing it are presented; as well as any issues or problems that might be encountered when using it.

Review your professional development

We are all at different stages in our development as teachers. But to achieve professional development goals we need to know where we are, where we want to be and how to get there.

---

1. **Plan goals for your professional development**
2. **Review your professional development**
3. **Review changes in your teaching**

Plan goals for professional development

Purpose: to develop a professional development plan

For many teachers, professional development is like the weather: it just happens, and, if you are lucky, it may happen somewhere near you. Most teachers don't get much of a say in shaping their own professional development. Or they don't *feel* that they have much of a say. That is perhaps a consequence of the way teaching has become – in many contexts – a kind of technical job, where the teacher's role is simply to "deliver" syllabus content according to pre-specified goals. This can have the effect of stripping teachers of a sense of their own "agency".

But if you talk to teachers who are further along in their career, you'll often find that they took deliberate steps to engineer their own development. (For me it was a three-in-the-morning moment, when I realized I *had* to do a masters course!) And that's what this tip is about: taking control of your professional development by setting your own goals and mapping out the steps that you will take to achieve them.

1 The teacher development life cycle: first of all, it's worth noting that teachers' professional lives tend to move in stages, and the goals you set yourself may vary depending on the stage you're at. In a classic study (Hubermann 1989), at least three stages were identified, along with the attitudes that characterize them:

1. Novice – surviving
2. Mid-career – stabilization, experimentation, taking stock
3. Late-career – serenity, disengagement

In a similar study, but specific to English language teaching, Garton and Richards (2008) came up with a four-stage trajectory:

1. Starting out
2. Becoming experienced
3. New horizons: professional development
4. Passing on the knowledge

You might like to plot yourself onto either of these cycles – where are you currently situated? How soon will it be before you are ready to move on?

The implication is that, if your goal is simply to survive from one lesson to the next, then you may not be giving much thought to professional development. Nevertheless, even novice teachers probably don't plan to tread water forever. Professional development has a lot to do with transitioning from one stage to the next.

2 Visualizing your ideal "teacher self": an important aspect of goal setting is having a clear "image" of who it is you want to be, professionally speaking, in the not too distant future. A theory of motivation that has implications here is what is called *the motivational self system*. Very simply, this proposes that we are motivated when we have a clear idea of who we would like to become (our "ideal self") and the steps that need to be taken in order to bridge the gap between our actual self and this ideal. It works best if this ideal self can be very clearly visualized.

Take some time to think about your "ideal professional self" in, say, five years' time. Which of these possible selves – if any – does it resemble?

- Running a small language school in an exotic location
- Working closely with learners with special needs in immigrant communities
- Training new teachers, using a method that you are confident in
- Teaching academic writing skills as preparation for university study
- Writing textbooks for use in the primary sector in developing countries
- Giving presentations at international conferences

If none of these "ideal selves" works for you, visualize your own. If possible, compare it with that of a colleague.

3 A road map for professional development: now, what steps will you need to take in order to achieve this goal? What support will you likely need? What kind of time frame are you looking at?

As you work through this book, you may want to made adjustments to your plan: that's OK; consider it 'work in progress'.

Garton, S., & Richards, K. (eds) (2008). *Professional Encounters in TESOL*: Discourses of Teachers in Teaching. Palgrave Macmillan.
Huberman, M. (1989). The professional life cycle of teachers. *The Teachers College Record, 91(1)*, 31–57.

Purpose: to assess your level of professional development

One thing that often strikes me is how different the field of language teaching today is from what it was like when I first entered the profession – last century. I am thinking not only of changes brought about by technology, but also of changes in what we know about language, about second language learning, and about language teaching. And today, teachers are expected not only to be both good at teaching, but also to be specialists in something – whether it be ESP, young learners, or blended learning. Language teaching is now recognized as a field of educational specialization. This is a very positive development since it reminds people that language teaching requires a specialized foundation of knowledge and skills that is obtained both through academic study and practical experience. (For a fuller elaboration of this knowledge and skills base see the reference at the end of this tip.) In this tip, the focus is on assessing where you currently are in your professional development, and identifying aspects of your development as a teacher you would like to focus on in the future.

1 Let's start with your current qualifications: which of these qualifications do you have?

- A certificate-level qualification in TESOL
- A certificate in a specialized domain (e.g. teaching young learners)
- A diploma-level qualification in TESOL
- An undergraduate degree in TESOL
- A graduate degree in TESOL
- Others

2 Do you plan to take an additional qualification? If so, talk to someone who already has that qualification – perhaps a colleague or a teacher you can talk to online. Ask questions like these:

- How useful is the qualification?
- How difficult was it to obtain?

- Is it best to study for it full time, part time, face-to-face, or online?
- What advice would he or she give you?

3 What areas of teaching are you most experienced in? What are three or four areas of teaching that you would like to become more familiar with? Now for the areas you identified, what activities do you think could best help you develop expertise in each area?

take a course   go on-line   team teach   read   observe another teacher   attend a workshop   classroom experience

4 What are your main responsibilities in your school or institution? What responsibilities would you like to focus more on in future?

5 What professional development activities do you make use of?

Read books and magazines   Write for publication
Design instructional materials   Attend workshops and conferences
Research my teaching   Take part in online forums   Belong to a
teachers' group / professional organization   Other

6 Discuss your answers to question 5 with a colleague, if possible. What did you learn from the discussion?

7 Prepare a one-page statement about your experience and expertise as a teacher, of the kind that you could include in a job application. What has worked well for you? What hasn't worked so well? What have been your most important learning opportunities in your career so far? Then, if possible, compare your statement with colleagues, and discuss.

Cambridge English Teaching Framework http://www.cambridgeenglish.org/teaching-english/cambridge-english-teaching-framework/

British Council https://englishagenda.britishcouncil.org/continuing-professional-development/

3 Review changes in your teaching

Purpose: to reflect on how you have changed as a teacher

Change is something we all experience in our teaching careers. Over time we become more confident. We acquire a lot of new knowledge and skills. And we develop a deeper understanding of ourselves and of our learners. Some changes may take a long period of time, while others may happen relatively quickly. However, change does not necessarily mean doing something differently; it can mean a change in awareness. It can be an affirmation of current practice or belief, and it is not necessarily immediate or complete. The purpose of this tip is to reflect on how you may have changed since you first started teaching, to consider what prompted changes you have made, and to identify changes you think you would like to make in the future.

1 Think about some of the ways you may have changed since you started your career as a teacher. Can you give an example of change related to some of these aspects of teaching?

- How you view your role in the classroom
- The kinds of teaching style you most often use
- Your beliefs about the role of grammar in language learning
- Your understanding of how learners can make their learning more effective
- Your approach to correcting learners' errors
- Your beliefs about the importance of a "native-speaker" accent

2 How have the changes you mentioned above affected your teaching practice? Can you give an example for each change?

3 You might like to compare your list with a colleague. How similar or different are you?

I used to spend a lot of time on correcting students' written work. These days, I believe it is more important for students to make use of peer feedback, using a checklist I give them.

4 Can you suggest three other examples of changes you have experienced since you started teaching, and how they have affected your teaching practice?

5 Change can result from different causes. From the list below, what do you think are the four most important ways of initiating a change in your understanding of your teaching? What can you learn from them? Is there anything you could add to the list?

- Self-discovery
- Feedback from students
- Feedback from a supervisor
- Trial and error
- Peer feedback
- Observing other teachers
- Collaborating with other teachers
- Attending a workshop
- Learning something from reading
- Researching my own classes

6 New Year resolutions: do you sometimes make resolutions at the end of a year about things you would like to happen during the coming months? Try an activity of this kind in thinking about changes you would like to make to your teaching, and how you might bring them about, as in the example from Hamed below. You might like to discuss your list with a colleague after you complete it.

Although I have several years' experience teaching in an Institute, I don't have a formal qualification. I want to take a Cert Course in the next year, and to be able to register for a course I first need to take the IELTS test. I have begun studying for the test on my own, and will also take an IELTS preparation course in a couple of months.

Bailey, K.M. (1992). The processes of innovation in language teacher development: What, why and how teachers change. In Flowerdew, J., & Hsia, S. (eds). *Perspectives on Second Language Teacher Education* (pp. 253–282). Hong Kong: City Polytechnic of Hong Kong.
Freeman. D. (1989). Teacher training, development, and decision making: A model of teaching and related strategies for language teacher education. *TESOL Quarterly 23(1),* 27–45.
Richards, J. C., Gallo, P., & Renadya, W. (2001). Teachers' beliefs and the processes of change. *PAC Journal 1(1),* 41–64.

Find out how you teach

We often have an "imagined" view of how we teach, but sometimes it may be rather different from the way our learners or our colleagues view us. Collecting information about our teaching can help identify our strengths as well as things we may wish to change.

4. Use lesson reports to monitor your teaching
5. Watch or listen to yourself teaching
6. Observe each other teaching
7. Keep a portfolio
8. Keep a journal

Use lesson reports to monitor your teaching

> **Purpose: to document your teaching practices by recording details of lessons after you teach**

We often use lesson plans when we prepare our lessons. However, while lessons sometimes develop as planned, unanticipated things also happen during lessons and they may in fact contribute to the effectiveness of lessons. Lesson reports record key aspects of what happened during a lesson, and can be used to review our teaching, to trigger reflection and evaluation, and to document effective and less effective teaching practices. They are particularly useful when a group of novice teachers are teaching a course and plan to meet regularly to review how they are using the course materials. Lesson reports could also form part of your portfolio.

A lesson report is normally completed shortly after the lesson, making use of a checklist or other form to guide your recollection.

A lesson report usually contains several kinds of information about a lesson:

- a list of the activities that were used for the different stages of a lesson, such as the opening, the teaching tasks, and the closing, and comments on how much time was spent on different activities;
- reflections on what worked well, what did not work well, and what might be done differently next time.

While a lesson report is not a completely accurate account of what occurred during a lesson, it can serve as a useful record of many features of the lesson – details that might otherwise not have been remembered. The frequency with which you want to complete a lesson report will depend on how useful the information is to you.

A lesson report can be prepared by an individual teacher or by a group of teachers who are teaching on the same course. A lesson report can be a report of a whole lesson or of specific features of a lesson (e.g. how grammar, vocabulary, pronunciation, or error correction was addressed during a lesson). See Appendix 1 for a lesson report form for use with a grammar lesson.

When teaching from a textbook, the report could be based on the exercises contained in a unit, together with additions you may want to make to the unit:

	How I carried out the activity	Time	Suggestions for next time
Exercise 1	..............................….........	….........	.............................….........
Exercise 2	..............................….........	….........	.............................…......... etc.

If the report focuses on a lesson plan based on a lesson you prepared yourself, the lesson plan provides the content for the main structure of the report. The report could be made through annotations to the lesson plan.

A lesson report could also focus on the kinds of teaching techniques or activities you made use of during lessons. For example, in a reading course a lesson report could list pre-reading, while-reading and post-reading activities.

Try it: develop a lesson report form that could be used to monitor the way pronunciation was addressed during a speaking course.

An alternative to a report form is to take a few minutes after a lesson to write an account of the lesson. The report could include both a descriptive account of the lesson, briefly summarizing how the lesson proceeded, as well as a reflective component in which you reflect on how well the lesson realized its aims and what you might do differently next time.

Watch or listen to yourself teaching

Purpose: to use a recording to observe how you teach

As teachers, we all tend to carry an idea of ourselves as a teacher. Our understanding of our teaching self tends to be a positive one, and hopefully it reflects the kind of teacher we really are. But it is difficult to get an objective view of our teaching self, as I discovered when I first started recording some of my lessons. In this tip, we consider what we can learn from making an audio or video recording of some of our lessons.

1 Planning for recording a lesson: decide if you will make one or more audio or video recordings of your lessons and consider the logistics involved. I have generally found that a series of recordings made during a term provide a good variety of information.

There are many ways of making a recording of a lesson including using a computer, smartphone or other audio device. You could have your students video your lessons or ask a colleague to make a recording.

There is advice on how to video-record your class in the reference at the bottom of the tip.

2 Focus of the recording: do you want to record a whole lesson or part of a lesson? Do you wish to focus on particular students or on the class as a whole?

3 Consult your students: explain your purpose to the students and check if they are happy for you to make recordings.

4 Rehearse and practice: to help the students become comfortable with the recording procedure and not be distracted or influenced by it, have a trial run to see if any difficulties arise and to make sure you are recording the kind of information you are interested in.

5 Choose what to record: decide on the specific focus of the audio or video recording. For example:

- how you communicate the goals of the lesson and of activities
- how you give instructions and feedback

- how you pace the lesson
- how you ask and answer questions
- how you establish rapport with the students
- how you use the classroom space
- how you use the textbook
- how you deal with classroom management issues
- how much teacher talk occurs in the lesson
- how actively the students are involved in the lesson.

Additional questions to consider when listening to or viewing a recording include:

- How loudly do I speak?
- Do I get off track at all? How often?
- Do I do anything annoying or distracting with my voice, gestures, posture, etc.?
- How do I use gesture and eye contact to complement my teaching?
- How clear are my instructions for activities?
- How clearly do I communicate the big ideas in a lesson?
- Am I interacting with students effectively?
- What are students doing as I'm speaking?
- Does my method of instruction seem appropriate for the content and goal I have in mind?
- How much time do I spend talking about things that don't need to be talked about?

6 Playback: when you listen to or watch the recordings, note both positive aspects of your teaching and anything you may wish to change or modify. You may also wish to share the video with a colleague and explore questions such as these:

- What do you think are the most positive features of the lesson?
- Was there anything that surprised or puzzled you?
- Can you suggest any alternatives I could try?

www.teachingchannel.org/videos/improve-teaching-with-video
http://education.temple.edu/ofp/step-one-record-your-lesson

Observe each other teaching   6

Purpose: to observe how another teacher teaches

Teachers don't always enjoy having someone observe them. I guess it's a normal reaction, but observing another teacher is a useful way not only of observing the teaching strategies another teacher uses, but also of prompting reflection on your own teaching. It also helps establish the idea of *a learning school* or collegial culture (see Tip 41) – sometimes referred to as *a community of practice*. This tip focuses on using observation to learn more about teaching rather than to evaluate teaching.

The purpose of observation in this activity is for the observer to watch a lesson and to collect information about the lesson that the teacher being observed would have difficulty collecting themselves.

1 Talk to a teacher who would like you to observe their class. Clarify that you will not be evaluating the lesson but collecting information about features that the teacher would like you to focus on.

2 Before you schedule a lesson to observe, find out as much as you can about the class you will watch. Discuss these and other questions:

- What kind of class is this?
- Who are the students? What is their level and do they have a similar ability level? What are their strengths and weaknesses?
- What teaching materials and other resources are being used?
- Are there any problems or difficulties with this class?
- What teaching approach does the teacher make use of?

3 As an observer, your task is to record information about features of the lesson. You could use:

- A checklist, e.g. of different question types, if that is the focus of the observation. (See Appendix 3.)
- A narrative: you simply write your account of the lesson as it unfolds, perhaps making notes against a timeline.
- A seating chart in which you check the number of times individual students ask or answer a question during the lesson.

4 The teacher identifies what they would like you to observe. These could be teacher behaviors, learner behaviors, or both. There should be some aspect of teacher or learner performance and participation that can be readily observed and recorded by the observer, such as the number of times students ask questions, i.e. low inference features, and not things that could not be observed but which depend on making inferences, such as whether the students found the activities useful – a high inference feature (see Tip 11). Useful examples could be:

- How much time the teacher spent on different aspects of the lesson
- The types of questions the teacher asked (see Tip 16)
- The way the teacher corrected learner errors
- The amount of student participation that occurred during the lesson
- The kinds of pronunciation or other errors made by learners
- The kinds of questions students asked

4 After the observation you should reflect on what you found most interesting about your colleague's lesson and teaching style. How does their teaching compare with the way you typically teach a lesson? Is there something you observed that you would like to try in your classes?

Discuss the information you collected with the teacher. Your role during this process is to be non-judgmental. However if the teacher asks you, "How did you like my teaching?" you should first comment on what you liked most about the lesson:

I really liked the way you set up the first activity.

If the teacher asks for suggestions, you could offer brief and constructive feedback, if appropriate. For example:

I wonder if the task might have worked better as a whole-class activity.

5 Arrange a time for the teacher to observe your class, and follow the same procedures.

Wainryb, R. (1993). *Classroom Observation Tasks: A Resource Book for Language Teachers and Trainers*. Cambridge: Cambridge University Press.
Yurekli, A. (2013). The six-category intervention analysis: a classroom observation reference. *ELT Journal 67(3)*, 302–312.
Carolan, L., & Wang, L. (2012). Reflections on a transnational peer review of teaching. *ELT Journal 66(1)*, 71–80.

Keep a portfolio

> **Purpose: to assemble a collection of items that illustrate your practice as a teacher**

A portfolio is a collection of items that you assemble to present an overview of your thinking and practice. The portfolio contains items that reflect who you are, the kinds of beliefs and thinking you make use of, your teaching skill and abilities, and how you are realizing or working towards your goals. Many teachers I have worked with find that keeping a portfolio is a very straightforward way of describing and reflecting on their work and achievements, and one which they find beneficial. As a teacher I worked with recently commented:

It gave me a chance to see how far I have come as a teacher since I started teaching.

This tip describes how to assemble a portfolio.

1 Decide on how you will make a portfolio: a portfolio could either be paper-based or digital. An electronic portfolio contains the same information as a paper-based one but is a multimedia approach allowing you to present the portfolio in a variety of formats, such as audio, video, graphics, and text. Hypermedia links are used to connect each section.

2 Decide on the purposes of keeping a portfolio: is it just for you or will you share it with colleagues or a supervisor? List all the different purposes you think would be important for you, for example: *to monitor my own practice, to contain examples of my students' work.*

3 Decide on the kinds of items to include in your portfolio. If the portfolio is to be shared with others, it would usually begin with an overview written by you to explain what the portfolio contains and why the items in it have been included. Each item would also be accompanied by an explanation of its importance. Finally, the portfolio will include a conclusion with reflections on what the collection means to you.

The following are examples of items that could be included:

a. A Teaching Philosophy Statement: this consists of a brief account of your approach to teaching and the beliefs and principles you bring to teaching. This could describe the kind of teaching you seek to achieve in your classes; how you view your role in the classroom; the kinds of learning you try to encourage and develop in your learners.

b. Documents that illustrate your approach to teaching. These could include:
- An up-to-date CV
- Sample course descriptions and syllabi
- List of courses you teach
- Samples of assignments
- Samples of materials and assessments you have prepared
- Samples of students' work
- Comments on your teaching by a peer or supervisor
- Student evaluations
- Photos of students carrying out activities in your classes
- Video of a class
- School activities such as committees you serve on, or mentoring you provide to new teachers
- Professional development activities you have participated in.

4 Using the portfolio: the portfolio is added to and updated on a regular basis. Once it is assembled, it can be used as a basis for reflection on your professional development. It can also be used when applying for promotion or when applying for a new teaching position.

Davis, J., & Osborn, T. A. (2003). *The Language Teacher's Portfolio: A Guide for Professional Development* (Contemporary Language Studies). Westport, CA: Praeger.
Bailey, K. M., Curtis, A., & Nunan, D. (2001). *Pursuing professional development: The self as source*. Boston, MA: Heinle & Heinle.

Keep a journal

Purpose: to use a journal to reflect on teaching

A teaching journal is a written account of your teaching experiences that can serve both as a record of things that happen during teaching, and also as a place to record reflections, incidents, questions, insights, and other comments that can be reviewed to better understand your teaching. Writing about teaching can prompt you to reflect on your teaching and enhance your awareness of the way you teach and how students learn, and it is also a simple form of classroom research. This tip examines the nature of journal writing and how it can be used.

1 Planning: a number of decisions have to be made when you undertake journal writing. How are you going to keep your journal? You can either use a notebook in which journal entries are written, or use an e-journal. Many teachers find blogs a useful approach to reflecting through writing. For example, I recently read a great blog about a teacher in Spain who was interested in teaching a semester without using a coursebook. He described how he got the students and school to agree, and documented the process.

Who is your audience? You need to decide who the primary audience is for the journal. Is it just for you, or do you plan to share it with others, such as colleagues or a supervisor?

What is your time frame for journal writing? Decide when is a good time for you to spend 10 or 15 minutes on journal entries.

2 Topics to write about: journal entries are both descriptions of things that occurred during lessons as well as reflections or interpretations of incidents or lessons.

Topics could include:
- the content of a lesson
- students' reactions to activities
- problems encountered with aspects of a lesson
- unanticipated incidents that occurred

- how materials were used
- effective moments during a lesson
- unsuccessful moments during a lesson.

Reflections and interpretations could include:

- explanations or understandings of classroom incidents
- examples of how principles and values were realized in a lesson
- understandings of how students' learn
- personal theories that account for aspects of learning
- accounts of changes in beliefs
- recognition of personal growth
- reflections on future goals

If you plan to share your journal with other teachers or a colleague, you may also pose questions for them to consider and respond to.

3 How to write: journal writing may take several forms. You may choose to write in note form or make your entries more of an extended narrative. Here is an example from a teacher in a Japanese university:

> 'Need to keep it stimulating for those guys who have lots of ideas'.
> Students had done a survey outside of class on meat eating and
> vegetarianism. The task of the class was to write a report on what they
> had found out, in a group of four, and then feed back their report to
> the whole class. While watching students perform this task I became
> strongly aware of the differences in levels within the class. When it
> came to listening to the feedback, the more able students were bored
> listening to their more hesitant classmates.

(Richards and Farrell 2005)

4 Using the journal: the journal can be used as a source of review and reflection. It can also serve as a record of how you teach and document some of the innovative and effective teaching practices you make use of. It could also be included in a teaching portfolio (see Tip 7).

Richards, J.C., & Farrell, T. S. C. *Professional Development for Language Teachers: Strategies for Teacher Learning.* Cambridge: Cambridge University Press.
Richards, J.C., & Belinda Ho, B. (1998) Reflective thinking through journal writing. In *Beyond Training.* Cambridge: Cambridge University Press.
Bailey, K. M., Curtis, A., & Nunan, D. (2001). *Pursuing professional development: The self as source.* Boston, MA: Heinle & Heinle.

Observe the nature of lessons

There are many different kinds of lessons but there are some features that are common to all effective lessons. Knowing what these features are can help with both the planning and the management of successful lessons.

9. Review designs for lesson plans
10. Identify the features of an effective lesson
11. Develop a lesson observation form

Review designs for lesson plans

> **Purpose: to consider the features of a lesson that should be included in a lesson plan**

Do you use a lesson plan when you teach? Is it a written plan or a mental plan? Mine is more often the latter unless I am teaching unfamiliar content or an unfamiliar class. In this tip, we will consider the features of a lesson plan and compare different formats for lesson plans.

1 What is the role of lesson plans? Do you agree with these statements?

- A successful lesson must follow a lesson plan.
- If you have a lesson plan you should follow it.
- You don't need a lesson plan if you are using a coursebook.
- Only novice teachers need lesson plans.
- A plan should start with the objectives of the lesson.
- A mental plan is better than a written plan.
- A detailed lesson plan is a restriction for a teacher.
- Teaching is a personal activity so it's better to plan lessons on your own.
- You can't teach from someone else's lesson plan.

These days, my planning consists of reviewing a lesson to anticipate problems and find ways of making it as interesting as possible for my learners. Most often I use a mental rather than a written plan.

2 Stages in a lesson: lessons usually consist of three stages – *the opening stage, the instructional stage, the closing stage.* The opening can help prepare learners for the lesson, the instructional stage is where the main teaching takes place, while the closing often serves as a brief review of the lesson. Can you suggest other purposes for the opening and closing phases of a lesson?

3 Lesson activities: consider one or more of the following scenarios and brainstorm the kinds of activities you could use for each stage of a lesson.

- Scenario 1 – a lesson on the past tense for basic-level learners
- Scenario 2 – a one-hour discussion class for students at advanced level
- Scenario 3 – a listening lesson using video clips of a news broadcast

4 Reviewing a lesson plan: look at this teacher's brief lesson plan for a lesson on the past tense. What is your opinion of the teacher's plan? Do you think it can be improved? If so, how?

1. Distribute a story with key verbs omitted.
2. Students try to guess the missing words.
3. Teacher reads the story. Students check their answers.
4. Teacher write up verbs from the story with both present tense and past tense forms.
5. Students complete sentences with past tense verbs.
6. Students receive another story. The sentences are in the present tense and are not in the correct order.
7. Students work in pairs to unscramble the story and to provide the correct past tense forms.

5 Preparing a lesson plan: now choose one of the other scenarios in 3 (or a lesson of your choice) and develop a lesson plan for it. Your plan should address these questions:

- Objectives. What will be the objectives of the lesson?
- Activities. What kinds of things will students do during the lesson, such as dialogue work, free writing, or brainstorming?
- Sequencing. What activities will be used for the opening, instructional, and closing stages of the lesson?
- Timing. How much time will be spent on each activity?
- Grouping. When will the class be taught as a whole, and when will they work in pairs or groups?
- Resources. What materials will be used, such as the textbook, worksheets, or internet?
- Evaluation. What procedures will be used to determine the effectiveness of the lesson?

What issues did you need to resolve? If possible, discuss your lesson plan with a colleague.

6 Evaluation of a lesson plan template: review the lesson plan template on page 114. How similar is it to the lesson plan format you developed? How useful would it be for your teaching context? Would you need to adapt it? What changes would you make to it?

Anderson, J. (2015). Affordance, learning opportunities, and the lesson plan pro forma. *ELT Journal 69(3)*, 228–238.

10 Identify the features of an effective lesson

Purpose: to consider the features an effective lesson

Good teaching is sometimes described as both a science and an art. It is a science in the sense that there are certain features of effective lessons that can be objectively identified through careful investigation and research. But teaching can also be understood as an art, since it also depends on the individual skill and creativity of the teacher, and this differs from one teacher to another. For me, while an effective lesson engages the students and provides opportunities for all the students to participate and learn, it also give the learners something they can take away from the lesson and makes the experience of coming to class worthwhile. In this tip we will explore ways of clarifying our understanding of the features of effective lessons.

1 Effective lessons you remember: think of an effective lesson that you taught or experienced recently. Why do you think it was successful? Look at the items on this list and add others of your own. Then rank the three most important features from 1 (most important) to 3. If possible, compare your answers with a colleague.

- The students enjoyed it.
- It moved at a good pace.
- It was well organized.
- It had a variety of different activities.
- It challenged the student, but not too much.
- It made connections with the students' lives and interests.
- There was a good atmosphere in the class.
- The content was relevant and interesting.

2 The rules behind a good lesson: when you teach, do you follow a set of mental "rules" or principles that guide the way you plan and teach the lesson? For me, two of my most important principles are "Learning English is hard work, but it can also be fun", and "Get out of the way as soon as possible and let the students do their thing".

What are three rules that you try to follow in your lessons? What experience or beliefs are they based on? Do you always refer to them or do you sometimes have to create a new one for a particular situation? If possible, discuss with a colleague. Are your rules similar?

3 Look at this list of different aspects of a lesson. Can you give one or more principles related to each feature? For example: 1) – *the teacher does not dominate the lesson.* If possible, compare your list with a colleague.

1) the role of the teacher in the lesson
2) the role of the students
3) the teacher's use of English
4) the students' participation
5) the students' use of English
6) the feedback the teacher provides to learners
7) the use of the textbook or other materials
8) the content of the lesson
9) the dynamics of the lesson
10) the class "climate" or atmosphere

4 Now choose the five most important principles you think account for a successful lesson. Then, for each principle, clarify in more detail how the principle can be realized in classroom practice, as in the example below:

Principle: *The lesson provides a success experience for learners.*

Realization: *Activities are at the right level and can be successfully completed by all the students in the class. When the lesson is over they feel a sense of having made progress.*

5 Skill-based lessons: what rules or principles do you refer to for skill-based lessons, such as a reading, writing, speaking or listening lesson? Here are some of my principles. Can you suggest two more core principles for each kind of lesson?

- a reading lesson: *the lesson teaches rather than tests reading*
- a writing lesson: *the lesson develops fluency as well as accuracy*
- a speaking lesson: *students get a maximum amount of talking time*
- a listening lesson: *the activities relate to real-world listening purposes*

If possible, discuss your ideas with a colleague.

11 Develop a lesson observation form

> **Purpose: to develop a form that can be used when observing a lesson**

Do you sometimes have the chance to observe other teachers' lessons? I find that there is always something useful I can learn when I watch another teacher teaching their class. However, it is useful to know what to look for in a lesson. In this tip the focus is on developing an observation form to observe your own or another teacher's lessons. (See Tip 6 for ideas on how to observe a colleague teaching.)

1 The observable features of a lesson: some aspects of a lesson can be observed (such as how many times the students ask questions), while some can only be inferred (e.g. whether the students understood the purpose of an activity). In developing an observation form, it is therefore important that it includes features of a lesson that can be observed and not features that can only be inferred. Look at this list of lesson features. Give examples of things that can readily be observed during a lesson in relation to each item on the list. For example:

the teacher's instructions: *the teacher used English to give instructions*
the teacher did not repeat explanations

- the teacher's instructions
- the teacher's questions
- the students' questions
- the teacher's explanations
- the activities the teacher makes use of
- the use of the textbook or teaching materials
- the teacher's use of technology
- the feedback the teacher gives to learners
- the teacher's use of time
- the teacher's use of classroom space
- the interaction between the teacher and the students
- the interaction among the students' themselves.

2 Developing an observation form: now use the features you selected to develop an observation form that a colleague could use to observe one of your classes. After you have tried out the observation form, make any necessary changes based on how well it worked.

3 An observation form for a particular type of lesson (e.g. a grammar lesson, a reading lesson): the lesson features discussed above are very general and reflect the features of any kind of lesson. Observation forms can also be developed for specific kinds of lessons, such as a grammar lesson or a reading lesson. For example, a reading lesson usually includes a pre-reading, while-reading and post-reading phase. Items in an observation form for the pre-reading phase could include:

- During the pre-reading phase, the teacher asked the students to preview the text by looking at the title of the text, the illustrations, and the headings, and to suggest three questions they thought the text might answer.
- The teacher activated students' background knowledge by asking questions related to the topic of the text and the type of text they would read.
- The teacher created an interest in the text they would read by linking it to current events or to the students' interests.
- The teacher introduced some key words that could present difficulty in the text.
- The teacher asked the students to identify a suitable purpose in reading a text of the kind provided.

4 Planning task: plan an observation form that covers a specific type of lesson that you teach. Ask a colleague to try it out by observing one of your lessons. After you have done so review the form. Do you need to make any changes to it?

5 Reviewing a lesson observation form: look at the observation form in Appendix 3 and consider these questions:

- How does it compare with the observation form you developed?
- Does it include only low-inference lesson features?
- How practical and useful is a detailed observation form of this type?
- Would this observation form be useful to observe one of your classes?
- Would you adapt it any way before you asked a colleague to use it in observing one of your classes?

Find out more about your learners

Learning is not necessarily the mirror image of teaching. Understanding how learners learn and the way they understand and approach their learning can help us provide better support for learning.

12. Identify your students' learning needs
13. Explore understandings of teaching and learning
14. Study examples of students' work
15. Learn from critical incidents

Identify your students' learning needs

Purpose: to prepare a profile of the learning needs of a class

Every English course aims to address the students' learning needs. Finding out what those needs are (i.e. conducting a needs analysis) is an essential aspect of designing a language course. Although in any class some students may have different needs from others, a well-designed course aims to address the most common needs the learners face. The aim of this tip is to develop a profile of the learning needs of a class of students so that your teaching can better address their needs. In this tip we will use the example of a reading course, but similar procedures could be used with other skills or areas of learning.

1 Find out what kind of reading students do: the first step is to generate a set of questions such as the ones below, and to find answers to the questions through needs-analysis procedures.

Out-of-class reading
- What kinds of things do the students like to read?
- What kinds of reading do they do outside of class?
- What kinds of texts do they need to read?

How they read
- How do the students typically read a text?
- How do they deal with unfamiliar vocabulary?
- Can they read for main ideas?
- Can they read and make inferences?
- Can they summarize the main points in a text?
- Can they choose a suitable reading strategy when they read a text?

Their main reading difficulties
- What are the students' main barriers to successful reading?
- Do they have a large reading vocabulary?
- Can they read authentic texts?

Classroom reading activities
- What kinds of reading activities work best with the students?
- What kinds of things do they like to read about?

- How long can they spend on a reading activity?
- Do they prefer print-based reading or online reading?

2 Needs-analysis procedures: a number of different methods can be used to find out about learners' needs. For example:

- test information on students' reading performance
- reports by teachers on typical problems students face
- information from students via interviews and questionnaires
- information from books and articles
- talking to teachers with relevant experience
- information from learner diaries and journals
- interviews with students
- observation of students reading
- analysis of the kind of texts students have to read
- a case study in which a student's reading experience is monitored over a period of time.

3 Identify learning aims: based on the information you got from asking questions such as the ones above, the next step is to describe the aims of the course, in this case a reading course. For example:

- To develop a reading vocabulary of 3,000 words.
- To be able to read a text quickly for gist.
- To scan a text quickly for facts and details.
- To read the main ideas with a good level of understanding.
- To read and identify the purpose of a text.
- To distinguish main ideas from supporting details in a text.
- To read and summarize correctly the main information in a text.
- To read and make appropriate inferences from a text.

4 Selecting reading activities to address the course aims: you can now select materials to address the aims that have been identified. For example:

Aim: To scan a text quickly for facts and details
Activities: Students are given a text that includes facts and details, and they complete a chart or graph based on the text.
Students check whether statements based on the text are true or false.

5 Other kinds of courses: look at the questions in 1. What questions could you ask if you are developing one of these courses?

a) a speaking course   b) a listening course   c) a writing course

Explore understandings of teaching and learning

> **Purpose: to find out about your teaching role and learners' preferred ways of learning**

Learners usually come to English classes with many years' experience of both classroom learning and out-of-class learning. As a result, they usually have a good sense of how best they learn, and the kinds of interaction they would like to have with their teacher and their classmates. As teachers we also have our own understanding of how a class should function to support learning. This tip focuses on exploring how we see our role in the classroom and how our learners like to learn.

1 Your role as a teacher: which of the occupations below do you think best describes how you see your role in the classroom? (You may suggest another occupation if there is one that better reflects your role as a teacher.)

actor   architect   artist   builder   captain   choreographer
coach   conductor   counselor   film producer   friend
guide   manager   scientist   trainer

2 How does the role (or roles) you identify with influence the way you conduct your class and interact with your students? Complete these statements then compare with a colleague, if possible.

I am somewhat of a _____, which means that I _____ .

I am also sometimes a _____, which means that I _____ .

3 How I see my classroom: it is also useful to think of metaphors to describe the kind of culture we try to create in the classroom. Do any of these metaphors capture the nature of a lesson in your classroom? How? If not, can you suggest metaphors that do?

a banquet   a concert   an expedition   a party   a play
a symphony   a sports match   a TV show   a voyage

4 If a visitor came to observe one of your classes, what principle or principles would they see in action?

I believe learning should be fun so I try to make lessons stress free.

I believe students can learn a lot from each other so I do a lot of group work.

5 Do your learners have preferences for how they like to learn? Find out by developing classroom activities in which students give their opinions about the typical classroom activities and routines you use in your teaching. Include statements like these:

agree   disagree

- I like to study with a textbook.
- In English class, I like to learn by reading.
- I think it is important to study grammar.
- I learn best when I memorize rules.
- I like the teacher to explain grammar rules.
- I like to memorize dialogs to improve my speaking.
- I like to do group activities with other students.
- I like learning through watching movies.
- It's best to look up unfamiliar words in the dictionary rather than try to guess their meaning.
- I like doing activities online to improve my English.
- I want to learn to sound like a native speaker.
- I think it's useful to learn songs in English.
- I like working with a partner to practice speaking.
- I like to translate words to help remember them.

6 Develop statements like the ones in question 5 to find out what your students believe about topics such as the ones below, and others that relate to the kinds of classes you teach. The statements can be the basis of group discussion among students. Students can then present their recommendations to the class. When discussing their recommendations, you can give your own beliefs and suggestions.

- How to improve reading (speaking, listening, writing)
- How to get the most out of class time
- How to master English pronunciation
- How to develop a larger vocabulary
- How to improve accuracy in spoken English
- How to learn from watching TV and movies
- How to learn from the internet

Study examples of students' work

Purpose: to explore with colleagues how students approach learning

A lot has changed about the way we respond to students' work. I can remember a time when I would return a student's homework with a grade and a few comments and never see it again. Now, when most work is submitted digitally, we have a fantastic resource for analysis, comparison, and professional development. Studying examples of work students produce can prompt reflection on the teaching practices that led to the work, problems students may have with different aspects of a course, or with the curriculum, and can complement information we get from other sources, such as test scores. In this tip we will examine how to collect and review examples of students' work.

1 Consider the role of the activity: what can we learn from studying students' work? Here is my list. Can you add ideas of your own?

- The difference between exceptional and average performance
- Difficulties posed by some learning activities
- The impact of teaching
- The nature of student thinking

2 Ideally, you would work with a group of colleagues who would like to collect and analyze examples of students' work. There are lots of different kinds of learning samples you can use for this activity. For example:

- video records of students completing different kinds of classroom tasks
- written work, such as essays
- student projects or assignments
- records of ESL learners' chatroom interactions.

Any kind of student output could be included provided that it can be used to reflect on the nature of the activity, its intended learning outcomes, what students demonstrate or have learned from it, and the kind of teaching support that preceded or followed the activity.

3 Distribute the students' work: one member of the group chooses a sample to focus on. The teacher who provided the sample gives information such as:

- the kind of class the work is from
- the kind of students in the class
- the nature of the assignment students were given
- how the students were instructed to complete it
- the teaching that preceded the activity the students were assigned.

At this stage, the purpose behind the assignment is not given nor the outcome that the teacher had expected to obtain.

4 Reflect on the work: group members now reflect on the piece of work they have received without making any judgment or evaluation of it. The focus is on describing what they see or what they can infer from the piece of work, and trying to understand it from the point of view of the student. Ask questions like these:

- What information can we extrapolate from the piece of work?
- Is there anything unusual, unexpected, or interesting about it?
- What does it suggest about the kind of thinking the student used?
- To what extent has the student understood the assignment?
- What difficulties do you think the student encountered?

The group's thoughts can be listed on the board for later discussion.

5 Clarification from the teacher: the teacher who provided the work sample now provides more information such as background information about the student, why the teacher chose this task or activity, and how they would expect a top student to perform. The group reflects further in the light of the information and asks questions.

6 Consider implications: the next stage involves considering the implication for classroom practice. Ask questions such as these:

- How would you evaluate the quality of the student's work?
- Could the student have been better prepared for the task?
- What kind of feedback would be appropriate to give him or her?

Learn from critical incidents   15

Purpose: to reflect on the significance of unanticipated classroom events

Sometimes an unexpected incident or event occurs during a lesson. For example, once when teaching a class of teenagers from Japan I asked students to work with a partner, and one student refused saying, "I don't want to. I hate pair work". While some incidents may have no longer-term significance, some can prompt insights into aspects of teaching and learning. These moments can be opportunities for new learning and hence can be referred to as *critical incidents*. This tip deals with the nature and role of incidents such as these.

1 Critical and non-critical incidents: it is important to understand the difference between a critical incident and incidents of other kinds. A critical incident provides potential for further learning. Check the list of incidents below and mark those that you think could be called critical incidents and those that are simply a normal classroom incident.

- Some students took longer to complete activities than others.
- A student refused to take part in a speaking activity.
- Some students arrived late to class.
- Many students were unable to complete an activity that I thought they could all manage.
- Some students made fun of another student's poor English.
- I had too much material planned for the lesson.

Now consider these two examples of comments from teachers taking part in an in-service course I taught recently.

I am a firm believer in group work and using group work was an important focus of my TESOL certificate course. However, early in my first assignment in an EFL context, when I asked the students to do group work activities, many of the students complained that they didn't think they were useful and that they didn't feel comfortable doing group work.

Recently I worked on correcting some serious pronunciation problems that some of my learners have. I thought I had 'fixed' the problem since I spent quite a bit of time and effort on it in class. However, a week later the students were making exactly the same mistakes, prompting me to think that my efforts had been a waste of time.

In the first example, the incident prompted the teacher to rethink the value of group work. The second caused the teacher to question the role of practice. For the incidents you marked as critical in the list above, what features of them justify calling them critical incidents?

2 Using examples of critical incidents: critical incidents can be a focus of several different kinds of professional development activities including a journal, a portfolio, a discussion group, or for conversation through chatrooms, forums, and other social media groups.

In considering critical incidents, use questions such as:

- Why was this incident significant?
- What were your thoughts or beliefs prior to the incident?
- How did you react at the time?
- What is your understanding of the reasons for the incident?
- What assumptions about teaching / learning does this incident raise?
- Would you react any differently if it happened again? Why or why not?

3 Focusing on critical incidents in a teacher-support group (see Tip 20): if possible, form a group of teachers who would like to explore some of the critical incidents that occur in their teaching. Decide on a time frame and how often the group will meet. For example, you may decide to monitor a course for a term or for a shorter period.

Make sure members of the group have a common understanding of what is meant by a critical incident. Share some examples and discuss.

Sharing experiences can be based on written accounts containing:

- a description of what happened
- analysis of why it happened
- reflection on what the teacher learned from the incident.

These can be read and discussed when the group meets.

Review the language you use in teaching

As teachers of English, we need to use classroom language that provides the right kind of support for the development of our learners' use of English. This requires an awareness of the kind of English we use when we teach.

16. Observe how you use questions
17. Observe how you give feedback
18. Use lesson transcripts to explore classroom language

Purpose: to observe the kinds of questioning strategies used in teaching

A common teaching strategy we all use is to ask questions. Questions can help create a classroom where genuine interaction and communication takes place and where learners have opportunities to extend their language resources. This tip shows how you can monitor the kinds of questions you use. As with Tip 5, this tip requires you to record one or more lessons or lesson segments and to review the recording to identify the kinds of questions you typically ask.

1 The functions of questions: questions serve many different functions in teaching. Can you add any other functions to this list?

- to check students' understanding of new content
- to check students' understanding of classroom procedures
- to elicit vocabulary and grammatical structures
- to create a positive classroom atmosphere
- to stimulate and maintain students' interest
- to encourage student participation
- to organize classroom procedures
- to provide feedback

2 Types of teachers' questions: research into the questions teachers ask has identified some main types.

- *Display vs. referential questions*: *Display questions* are used to check understanding or to elicit information from learners. For example: "How do we pronounce this word?" *Referential questions* are "real" questions and require the student to give information, give an opinion, or explain something. For example: "How did you enjoy the movie?"
- *Closed vs. open-ended questions*: *Closed questions* tend to focus on recall of information and are typically display questions. They have only one acceptable answer and often produce short answers, not requiring higher-level thinking or extended responses. Teachers often use a succession of questions of this type to encourage

class participation and to develop aural skills and vocabulary. For example: "How many of you are social media?" *Open-ended* questions have many different answers and responses that may be longer than those of closed questions. They often require higher-level thinking, require students to give individual responses, and hence can elicit real communication and interaction. For example: "Why is social media so popular, do you think?"

- *Immediate response vs. delayed response*: Teachers usually expect an immediate response, but some questions allow a bit of thinking time before answering.

3 The effect of teachers' questions: there is a school of thought that a higher ratio of referential and open-ended questions improves the quality of communication in the classroom by increasing engagement and participation, as well as stretching learners' use of language. Also, research suggests that when students are given a longer time to respond, their answers are longer and more accurate, and failure to answer occurs less. It is also important that questions are evenly distributed, and that all students get a chance to answer.

4 Monitoring your use of questions: review a recording of a lesson and identify the kinds of questions you used. Check the extent to which you used questions for these purposes:

- for classroom management
- to generate interest in a topic
- to prepare students for an activity
- to check understanding
- to elicit language practice
- to increase participation in the lesson
- to increase motivation

Now identify the kinds of questions you asked. For example:

- What was the approximate ratio of display vs. referential questions? And of closed vs. open-ended questions?
- How much response time did you typically allow?
- How evenly distributed were your questions?

http://esol.britishcouncil.org/content/teachers/staff-room/teaching-articles/asking-questions

17 Observe how you give feedback

> **Purpose: to observe the kinds of learner feedback you give in teaching**

Providing learners with feedback about their learning is an important aspect of teaching. Feedback serves a number of functions. One is motivation. Positive feedback can help support students' efforts to communicate and try out what they have learned. Another kind of feedback is responses to students' use of English. This kind of feedback is intended to facilitate learning. As with Tip 5, this tip requires you to record one or more lessons or lesson segments (or to invite a colleague to observe your class), and to review the recording to identify the kinds of feedback you typically provide.

1 Recognizing different kinds of feedback: review your recording and notice how you gave these kinds of feedback:

- *Motivational feedback.* This serves to encourage learners to take risks and to try out new words, grammar or expressions. This can be achieved with expressions of praise such as "Good", "Right", "Excellent answer", "That was a nice dialog", "Thanks", "I liked the way you said that", "Excellent pronunciation".
- *Feedback on form.* This type of feedback draws the students' attention to the accuracy of what he or she has said. However, it is important that feedback on form does not discourage students from attempting to communicate. It should not lead to embarrassment or loss of face. It can be either direct or indirect.
- *Direct feedback.* This refers to explicit correction of a student's error. For example:

   Can you say that again using the past tense?
   I didn't hear the final sounds on some of your words.
   Can someone correct that answer from Tony?
   What word should Anna have used in the first exercise?
   Can you say it again with the correct word order?

- *Indirect feedback*. This is an alternative to directed feedback, and can be achieved in a number of ways:
  - by repeating what the student says using tone of voice to indicate that something was not correct
  - by providing examples of incorrect statements or utterances and asking students to say why they are incorrect
  - by indicating that you did not understand something, prompting the learner to try to say it in a different way
  - by rephrasing an utterance and correcting it. This is known as *recasting*. Research suggests that recasts are an important source of learning for many language learners.

> S: I arrive three weeks ago.
> T: Oh, you **arrived** three weeks ago.

2 Reflect on the way you gave feedback: consider these questions as you review the feedback strategies you used.

- What were your goals in giving feedback? Was it to motivate, to correct, or to encourage learners? Was the balance appropriate?
- How effective is your motivational feedback? Do you give too little or too much? If you changed the way you gave motivational feedback, how would it affect your teaching?
- Do you give a balance of direct and indirect feedback on learners' errors? Can you vary the way you provide both kinds of feedback? If you use a lot of indirect feedback, are learners aware that you are trying to correct their use of English? If not, how could you make them more aware of it?
- Is the feedback you give clear and practical? "You need to improve your pronunciation," does not help learners; however, "Pay attention to your final consonants," draws attention to a specific problem. What are some ways in which your feedback could be made more practical?
- What kind of feedback do learners prefer? For example, do they think feedback is useful? How and when would they like it to be given?
- What is the effect of feedback on learners? Does it discourage them? If so, how can you give feedback in a fun and friendly way?
- Are you consistent in the way you give feedback so that students recognize feedback when you provide it? How could you make it more consistent?

18 Use lesson transcripts to explore classroom language

Purpose: to explore how language is used in teaching

This tip makes use of transcriptions of lesson segments as a basis for exploring features of teacher–student interaction, for language awareness, or to illustrate teaching procedures.

1 Choosing a lesson segment: to obtain usable lesson segments you can use recordings made for other purposes or arrange to film segments of the kind you are interested in. These segments should be relatively short; a segment of a few minutes duration can provide useful information. Depending on the focus of the activity, worksheets can be prepared as a basis for group activities.

2 Transcribing: a transcript is now made of the recording. Here is an example of a transcript showing how a teacher carried out the opening section of a literature lesson.

T: The other time we were talking about figures of speech. And we have already in the past talked about three kinds of figures of speech. Does anybody remember those three types? ... Mary?

S: Personification, simile, and metaphor.

T: Good, Let me write those on the board. Now can anyone tell me what personification is all about again? ... Juan?

S: Making a non-living thing like a person.

T: Yes. OK. Good enough. Now what about simile? ... OK. Cecelia?

S: Comparing two things by making use of words "like" or "as".

T: OK. Good. [Teacher writes the definition on the board] The other one – metaphor. Paul?

S: It's when we make a comparison between two things, but we compare them without using words such as "like" or "as".

T: All right. Good. So it's more direct than a simile.

---

3 Using the transcript: transcripts such as these can be used in different ways. For example, they can be used to explore how teachers ask questions, to give feedback, to provide explanations and examples, and the patterns of teacher–student interaction that occur in a lesson. What aspects of teacher–student interaction are illustrated in the segment above?

4 Here is an example of the use of a lesson transcript (adapted from Cullen, 2002):

Purpose: to explore the kinds of questions teachers used in presenting a reading text and to provide examples of how to use a reading activity, i.e. both as a language awareness activity as well as to demonstrate teaching methodology.

Resource: a transcript of part of a reading lesson.

Procedures:

- The participants listen to the recording and follow it using the lesson transcript.
- They take part in reading it aloud, working in pairs or as a whole class activity, with one person reading the part of the teacher and the others reading the students' lines.
- Participants receive a worksheet which gives a list of different types of questions and examples (see Tip 16). They then review the transcripts to identify and reflect on the kinds of questions the teachers used. Would their own practice be similar?
- Teachers now receive another transcript, but one in which the teacher's questions have been partially deleted. Sufficient words or phrases are provided so that the participants can try to guess what the missing questions are. For example:
  What .... the next paragraph is going to be about?
  Which part .... contains the topic sentence?
- The participants listen to the recording and compare their answers.
- The teachers now take part in a planning activity in which they plan a lesson around a reading text and consider how they would organize the different stages of the activity.

Cullen, R. (2002). The use of lesson transcripts for developing teachers' classroom language. In Trappes-Lomax, H., & Ferguson, G. (eds.) *Language in language teacher education* (pp. 219–238). Amsterdam: John Benjamin.

Engage in critical reflection

Learning from our own experiences as teachers is an important aspect of professional development. Processes of critical reflection can be used to explore who we are as teachers, as well as the understandings and beliefs that underlie our practice.

19. Learn how to engage in critical reflection
20. Take part in group problem solving
21. Use clips from movies or extracts from fiction to explore teaching
22. Try doing something differently

Learn how to engage in critical reflection

Purpose: to acquire the skills involved in critical reflection

In thinking about our professional development, we often assume that it involves taking workshops or doing courses. But if we think of professional development as bringing about changes in our understanding of teaching, this can often come about from thinking through and reflecting on our own teaching. In this tip we consider the nature of critical reflection and the types of activities that promote it.

1 The nature of critical reflection: critical reflection can be thought of as a three-step process:

- examining a teaching situation or experience
- asking questions about the purpose, meaning, and consequences of teaching actions and events
- rethinking beliefs and understandings in the light of new awareness and knowledge.

For example, as a student teacher I once got the sense that some of my lessons were not as engaging as they could be. Was it the materials? Was it the tasks? Was it the students? I audio-recorded a couple of lessons and after reviewing the tapes, decided it boiled down to the fact that I was "over-teaching" – spending too much time modeling and explaining, often saying the same things several times. This prompted me to ask myself why I was doing this and how I could conduct my lessons in a different way.

My example illustrates that critical reflection is based on the idea that experience in itself does not necessarily lead to greater levels of understanding. In order for experience to produce learning, it needs to be coupled with the process of reflection.

2 Phases in critical reflection: critical reflection involves asking different kinds of questions about teaching experiences.

- Mapping: What do I do as a teacher?
- Informing: What is the meaning of my teaching? What did I intend?
- Contesting: How did I come to be this way? How was it possible for my present view of teaching to have emerged?

- Appraisal: How might I teach differently?
- Acting: What and how shall I now teach?

3 Planning for critical reflection: critical reflection can be both an individual or a group-based activity. (Tip 22 gives examples of things you can do on your own.) Here are some examples:

A group of teachers who are interested in exploring their teaching collaboratively get together. During a first meeting, the group decides on procedures and topics. Procedures that can be used include lesson reports, journal writing, case studies, narratives, critical incidents and video recording (see Tips 4, 5, 8, 15, 32, 37 and 40).

The group decides on topics they want to explore. These could include:

- giving feedback on learner performance
- maintaining student engagement in lessons
- teaching styles.

The group brainstorms around the topic they have chosen and generates as many questions as possible related to the topic. For example:

- What issues does it involve?
- What do you think is the best strategy or practice?
- What problems have you encountered?

Group members then decide how they will collect information related to the topic and over what time frame. Discussion can focus around the issues noted above.

After completing a cycle of activities of this kind, participants reflect on what they learned from it:

- Was there anything surprising you learned about your own teaching?
- Would you wish to change any aspects of your teaching?
- How would you go about it?
- How useful was the experience of reflecting on your teaching in this way?

Gun, B. (2011). Quality self-reflection through reflection training. *ELT Journal, 65(2)*, 126–135.
Richards, J.C., & Belinda Ho, B. (1998). Reflective thinking through journal writing. In *Beyond Training*. Cambridge: Cambridge University Press.
Walsh, S., & Mann, S. (2015). Doing reflective practice: a data-led way forward. *ELT Journal 69(4)*, 351–362.

Take part in group problem solving

20

> **Purpose: to form a group that meets to reflect on and resolve issues and problems**

Do you remember the proverb "Many hands make light work"? It stresses how doing something with the help of others often works best. This is true in teacher development where group-based interaction is often an effective way of solving a problem. This is the focus of this tip.

1 Learning in a group: like other group-based activities, the group aims to draw on the members' collective knowledge, understanding, and experience to explore teaching issues, to develop new understandings of teaching, and to seek to resolve problems. Members of the group interact in a friendly and supportive way and respect each other's points of views and ideas, functioning as a "critical friend" who gives constructive feedback to support change and solve problems.

2 Participants: groups typically form on a voluntary basis and consist of teachers with shared interests and concerns, and who enjoy collaborating with other teachers to help resolve or clarify shared teaching concerns. A critical friends' group usually consists of a presenter, one teacher who serves as the facilitator, and up to six or seven group members.

3 Procedures: the group decides when and how often to meet. The format of a group meeting typically involves a teacher presenting an issue or dilemma to the group, and describing the practices he or she employs to address the issue. This could involve an examination of contributing factors that may influence the outcomes of the practice, such as the school culture, available resources, examples of students' work and anything else relevant to understanding the issues.

4 Issues and topics: the group can discuss any topic that members would like to have their input on. For example:

- dealing with reluctant learners in a class
- teaching creative writing with low proficiency learners
- using collaborative learning techniques in a writing class.

5 The format of a group meeting: although critical friends' groups can be organized in different ways, the following is an example of how a group functions.

- The teacher who is presenting identifies the topic or issue they will present and for which they would like the group's input. For example: "How to make effective use of a short story to stimulate critical and creative thinking on the part of students".
- The teacher assembles the necessary materials and resources that will be made available to group members during the meeting.
- Prior to the group meeting, the presenter and the facilitator meet to plan the presentation and choose any resources or examples of students' work that the presenter will discuss. During this conversation, the presenter and facilitator discuss the kinds of questions that the problem or work practice poses, and identify the issues that will be the focus of the group discussion. They also agree on a format or protocol to structure the discussion.
- At the group meeting, the presenter first presents an example of student work they would like the group to discuss. For example, in relation to the problem above, the group may receive a copy of the story and examples of things students produced as a response to the story, such as poems, illustrations, etc.
- The facilitator then leads the group through a series of discussions of the work, during which individual group members comment on or pose questions about the piece of work, such as the skills or knowledge it is intended to develop, the level of learner engagement it might elicit, the accuracy of the work, and so on. During this phase, the facilitator may guide the discussion, posing questions or clarifying and summarizing members' contributions.
- Following the discussion, the group explores how effective the meeting was in helping resolve the issue the teacher had presented.

Poehner, P. (2011). Teacher learning through critical friends' groups. In Johnson, K.E., & Golombek, P. R. *Research on Second Language Teacher Education* (pp. 189–203). NY: Routledge.
Vo, L. T., & Nguyen, H. T. M. (2010). Critical friends group for EFL teacher professional development. *ELT Journal 64(2)* 205–213.

Use clips from movies or extracts from fiction to explore teaching

21

> Purpose: to explore aspects of teaching with colleagues through watching movie extracts and reading extracts from fiction

Do you have any favorite movie scenes that depict teachers, or memorable descriptions of teaching incidents in fiction? One of mine from the movies is the scene in *Dead Poets' Society* where – in order to encourage non-conformism – the teacher, played by Robin Williams, gets up onto the desk and urges his pupils to do the same. Clips such as these from movies or TV shows can be a useful way of provoking a discussion about such things as: public perceptions of teaching (as projected by Hollywood); teacher's roles, e.g. teachers as performers versus teachers as instructors; classroom discipline; classroom dynamic; rapport; use of the classroom space, and so on. This tip focuses on working with a group of colleagues using movie clips in this way.

1 Recalling favorite teachers from shows: ask everyone in the group to recall a favorite or memorable teacher from a movie or TV show. Here are some things teachers came up with recently when they used this activity:

For me, I loved Mr. Garrison, South Park Elementary's fourth grade teacher in South Park. He may not be receiving a "teacher of the year" award any time soon, but Mr. Garrison is definitely one of South Park's most unusual and memorable residents.

How about the teacher Mr. Schue in "Glee"? He's a teacher who takes the responsibility of enriching the lives of his students very seriously, but we also get to see what his own life is like outside of the classroom.

The teachers in the Korean comedy "Please Teach Me English" are hilarious and a great example of how NOT to teach pronunciation.

This can lead into an interesting discussion of the kind of qualities teachers in movies or TV shows often depict. What is the stereotypical teacher like in these shows? Where do these stereotypes comes from?

2 Finding suitable clips: this is a group-based activity, so the next step is for the group to suggest some of their favorite teacher or classroom scenes from movies or TV shows. For example, on *Best Teacher Movie Moments* there are short trailers from movies depicting teachers.

(https://www.youtube.com/playlist?list=PL984C863D5D92FAFA)

3 Discussing the clips: when using a clip as a basis for reflection on teaching try watching the clip several times, each time focusing on a different kind of question. The questions will depend on the clip, but can serve to prompt ideas on issues such as these:

- What teacher qualities are depicted?
- How do the students view the teacher?
- What kind of interaction takes place between the teacher and the students?
- What assumptions about teaching and learning does the clip seem to be making?
- What would you change if you could re-shoot this scene – e.g. to make it more realistic?

A similar activity could be based around extracts from novels and memoirs which feature scenes of language learning and teaching. Here, for example, is an extract from the novel *Nowhere Man* by Aleksandar Hemon, where the protagonist is visiting an ESL school in Chicago. A classroom discussion is in progress:

> "When I had been a little child, I had had a friend who had had a big head ... Every child had told him about his big head and had kicked him with a big stick on his head. I had been very sad," Mihalka said, nodding, as if to show the painful recoil of the big head.
>
> "We are learning Past Perfect," the teacher said to us, and smiled benevolently ...
>
> "I must know Past Perfect," Mihalka said, and shrugged resignedly, as if Past Perfect were death and he were ready for it.

As a group activity, members can suggest similar scenes that warrant reflection through posing questions. For example:

- What message is the student trying to give?
- What is the teacher's message?
- How could an incident like this be considered as a critical incident? (See Tip 15.)

Try doing something differently

22

Purpose: to reflect on teaching by changing the way we usually do things

Much of our teaching is often based on fixed routines and procedures that we acquired in our initial teacher training. Doing things regularly in the same way helps them become almost automatic. We no longer have to think so much about them, and we can shift our attention to other dimensions of the lesson. This is generally a good thing, but from time to time it is worth breaking out of our routine and doing things differently in order to reflect on and evaluate the way we teach. Sometimes, breaking a routine may simply lead us to affirm our normal practice. At other times, however, it may prompt us to rethink the assumptions we hold about some of the things we typically do when we teach. This tip focuses on doing things differently as a way of prompting reflection and review.

1 An example of a changed way of teaching: a sequence of activities we often use in presenting a new item of grammar or a function is the P–P–P lesson sequence: *Presentation, Practice, Production*. In the Production phase, we encourage leaners to try out a new form, to experiment with it and extend its use. This obviously makes sense with very low-level learners who don't yet have the resources to engage in free production. But consider how we could change this sequence of events and use a different sequence with higher-level learners:

- Production – students are given a task or activity (e.g. a role play) and complete it as best they can. Based on their performance, the teacher identifies some of the language they need for a better performance of the task.
- Practice – the students repeat the task one or more times and, as they are trying it out, the teacher gives them some of the words and expressions that they need.
- Presentation – as a follow up, the teacher and the students analyze the task and the difficulties that arose as they performed it. The teacher gives an explicit account of the language demands and

features of the task and the "rules" that it reflects. Students may now be given another task of the same kind to practice.

What do you think are the advantages of presenting the activity in the way described above? Are there any disadvantages?

2 Considering alternatives: here are different ways of conducting some common classroom activities and procedures. What might be the advantages and disadvantages of each procedure?

- The teacher conducts the entire lesson without speaking, using gestures and actions to manage the class.
- The teacher teaches a unit from the textbook but in the reverse order.
- The teacher asks the students to read a short text aloud but to read it word by word backwards.
- In a speaking class, the students have to sing the dialogs rather than speak them.
- In a speaking class, rather than using the textbook, the teacher asks five students to place an item each on the teacher's desk. The lesson is built entirely around the items.
- Students take turns presenting the lesson, while the teacher watches from the back of the room.

3 Thinking of alternatives: choose three typical teaching procedures or activities that you often use. How could you change the way you use them?

Carry out the changed procedure and consider these questions:

- How did the change affect the way the activity worked?
- Did it have any benefits for the learners?
- What other benefits did it have?
- Were there any disadvantages in doing it this way?

Fanslow, J. (1987). *Breaking Rules*. Longman

Expand your knowledge of the field

Language teaching draws on a huge body of theory, research and practice and it's important to keep up to date with developments that are relevant to your teaching situation and background. There are many ways in which this can be accomplished.

---

23. **Form a reading group**
24. **Learn from an expert**
25. **Join a language teachers' association**
26. **Attend a conference**

---

23 Form a reading group

Purpose: to promote collaborative critical reading of professional articles and books

Have you read a professional book recently that gave you useful new ideas and information? I still remember one of the first books I read when I began my learning as a teacher – Close's *English as a Foreign Language* – which really changed my understanding of the nature of English. Reading is an important source of professional development, and reading well-chosen articles and books can help keep you up to date with developments in language teaching as well as provide ideas that you can apply in your practice. The first thing I did when I established a new English department at a university in Hong Kong was to set up reading groups. This tip draws on this experience and describes how reading can be more engaging if it is a collaborative activity. It can also help you read articles that are of potential interest but that may not always be written in an accessible style.

1 Form a group: find colleagues who are interested in developing their knowledge through reading. Members of the group identify suitable articles or books to read. In the case of articles, the group can look at abstracts of articles and decide which ones they would like to read.

2 How to read collaboratively: there are a number of ways of using group-based reading:

- "Unpacking" an article or book chapter. The group receives an article to read. Prior to the group meeting, two members of the group are asked to identify the main idea of the article and to develop some questions that will be used as a basis for discussion when the group meets. One of the members of the group prepares a summary of the discussion that is distributed to group members.
- Debating points of view. Two articles with strongly differing points of view on a topic are distributed to the group. Half of the group members read one article closely and skim the other article. The other members of the group do the same in reverse. When the group meets,

they prepare for a short debate. Each of the two groups meet to discuss their article, to prepare their points of view and to anticipate arguments from the other team. This may take up to 20 minutes depending on the nature of the article. The teams then have a debate, chaired by one of the group. During the debate they argue the point of view of the article they read. Following the debate there is a general discussion during which members give their own ideas on the issue.

- Agree or disagree. An article presenting a strong or controversial point of view is distributed. Group members work in pairs to write a letter in which they strongly agree or disagree with the point of view in the article. Members then exchange their letters, following which they have a discussion and share their own ideas on the issue.

- Editor's choice. An article of interest is distributed to the group, however the title of the article is deleted. In pairs, group members:
  - prepare an engaging title for the article,
  - suggest illustrations that could be used to make the article more visually appealing,
  - prepare an announcement about the article as if it was going to appear in a forthcoming issue of a journal or magazine.

The group then shares their suggestions, following which they give their reactions to the article.

- Reporters. Divide the group into two. One group consists of reporters and will interview the other group, who are the authors of the paper.

- True or false. Divide the group into two. Members of one group prepare a set of true/false statements based on the article. When the group next meets they read their questions and the other group has to decide if the statements are true or false.

- Poster. Each group has to imagine the author (or authors) of the paper is going to be the main speaker at an important conference. They prepare an engaging poster that highlights some of the key messages from the paper.

- Visuals. Pairs of teachers create visuals based on the article which they bring to a meeting and compare.

Fenton-Smith, B., & Christopher Stillwell, C. (2011). Reading discussion groups for teachers: connecting theory to practice. *ELT Journal 65(3)*, 251–259.
Wright T., & Bolitho, R. (2007). *Trainer Development*. Privately published.

24 Learn from an expert

> **Purpose: to learn from an experienced practitioner through a focused interview**

Do you sometimes recall memorable conversations you have had with other teachers? Once, I thought I would try using an extract from a play as a teaching resource and couldn't find a way of making it come alive for my students. I was on the point of giving up when my colleague Dino, who has a background in literature and drama, stepped in and gave me some great ideas on how to use the text. Of course, all schools contain teachers with a great amount of expertise and experience and it's good to find ways of tapping into it. One way to benefit from the expertise of other teachers or other specialists is to engage in a focused conversation through the use of a semi-structured interview as a professional development activity. This tip examines the nature and benefits of this activity.

1 Justification: while you can learn a lot from reading about a topic, an interview allows for focused, extended conversation and interaction. Information can be exchanged both ways and follow-up questions can be used to extend the discussion and clarify understanding. You can record the information and use it as a basis for reflection and application. In some cases, the interview could be conducted online and projected live into the classroom. It could also be relayed to all participants online, e.g. in the form of a webinar.

2 Subject of an interview: in every school or district there are teachers who have specialized knowledge on areas of their expertise, such as assessment, technology, or teaching adults, and they are often happy to share it with others. Visiting experts often visit schools and may be willing to share their expertise and answer questions. An interview is an informal way of learning more about a topic and also enables you to appreciate other teachers' specialized skills in your institution.

3 Format of the interview: semi-structured interviews are a flexible approach to interviewing. Topics and questions are planned in advance and used to guide the interview and to keep it focused; however, other topics and questions may arise allowing for more information to emerge.

4 Preparing for the interview: contact the person you would like to talk with and explain the purpose of the interview. The interview would normally take between 30 minutes and an hour. Ask if they are willing to let you record them, and explain how the information obtained will be used – either to improve your own knowledge, to help you resolve issues, to help prepare for a new teaching situation, or to share with other teachers in a group meeting.

Prepare the topics and questions you would like to discuss. For example, if you are unfamiliar with teaching adults, your list might include questions like this:

- How do adult learners differ from younger learners?
- What kinds of activities do they enjoy?
- How can you determine their needs?
- What sort of content works best with adults?
- Do they enjoy pair and group activities?
- What are some typical problems that occur with adult classes?
- What feedback methods do you recommend?
- Is it useful to let students use the mother tongue in class?
- What are some ways courses can be organized?
- What advice can you give to help me prepare for teaching adults?

Be prepared to ask other questions that occur during the interview, and to ask follow-up questions to obtain further information.

5 During the interview: decide if you will record the interview or take notes. These can be elaborated more fully after the interview.

6 After the interview: review your notes or the recording, make any additions to the notes, and write a summary of the information you obtained during the interview. This will serve both as a reference and reminder, but could also be included in a teaching portfolio.

7 Share with others: there may be other teachers interested in the results of your interview. If so, use your summary as the basis for a group meeting.

Join a language teachers' association

Purpose: to appreciate the benefits of belonging to a
professional organization

An important source of professional development for teachers is
through membership of a professional association. There are many
professional organizations for language teachers – such as TESOL
(Teachers of English to Speakers of Other Languages, an international
organization based in the US, with over 100 worldwide affiliates),
IATEFL (International Association of Teachers of English as a Foreign
Language, an international organization based in the UK), and JALT
(the Japan Association for Language Teaching). This tip describes what
such organizations do and the benefits of membership.

1 Functions of teacher organizations: the following are some of the
things language teacher associations (LTAs) do. Rank them in terms of
their interest to you, then compare with a colleague, if possible.

- enable networking and sharing information with other teachers
- organize conferences and workshops
- publish magazines or journals for teachers
- support research
- enable teachers to share information with others
- offer courses, seminars, workshops, and lectures
- provide information about trends in the field
- take public positions on important issues
- help raise the standards of the profession
- provide online forums and chat groups for teachers
- provide job information and career advice
- host websites for members
- provide resources that teachers can use

2 What teachers say about the benefits of joining LTAs:

I love to get the newsletter. It's full of useful teaching tips.

For me, the highlight of my school year is attending an IATFL conference. The conference for me is not just social. And it's not just academic. It's this building of a network of people who understand your thought processes and get you. It's part of my identity as a teacher, as a teacher trainer and as a person.

The TESOL affiliate that I belong to keeps me in the loop about the issues that I'm passionate about. By providing me with the latest news and research, I stay on the cutting edge of education which means that my students benefit from all the research out there that I would never have time to find on my own. I also love having a place to turn to when I have a question.

3 Interest groups: most LTAs offer members the chance to join a special interest group. Which three interest groups below would you be most interested in?

___ Business English ___Materials writers ___Young learners ___ ESP
___Pronunciation ___Learning technologies ___Literature ___Research
___Teacher training ___ Assessment ___ Blended learning

Now check out and compare the special interest groups available through IATEFL at http://www.iatefl.org/special-interest-groups/introduction

4 Other benefits: membership of a LTA also provides an opportunity to participate in conferences and workshops, to share teaching tips and materials with other teachers through newsletters and blogs, to review textbooks and other publications, and to serve as a volunteer and help organize seminars, workshops, and talks for members.

5 Deciding on what LTA to join: there are many different professional organizations for language teachers, so you need to consider which ones best fit your needs. Consider these questions when making a decision:

- What benefits does it offer me?
- Does it fit my needs?
- How it can it support my teaching?
- How can it support my professional development?
- What services does it offer?
- What demands will it make on my time?
- Is the price of membership affordable?

26 Attend a conference

Purpose: to learn the benefits of conference participation

There are numerous language-teaching conferences held in different parts of the world, some with a particular focus (such as Content and Language Integrated Learning or CLIL), and others providing a forum for presentations on many different kinds of issues. Participating in a professional conference offers many different kinds of learning opportunities for us, and can also be motivating and help us maintain our passion for teaching and keep up to date with trends and issues in the profession. This tip contains suggestions for getting the most out of conference participation.

1 Find out about conferences: find out what kind of conferences and other professional meetings are available in your location. Many conferences require registration in advance. Some offer on-site registration but sometimes at a higher rate than pre-registration.

2 Plan in advance: preview the conference program and think about the sessions that you would most like to attend and people you would like to meet. For example:

- keynote addresses (by a well-known person, whose talk may be primarily motivational or designed to open up new avenues of thought)
- plenary sessions by specialists – addressing the main themes of the conferences
- panel discussion where a group of speakers discuss a topic
- parallel sessions by teachers and researchers in which they share their work
- poster sessions – short poster-based displays of work by teachers and of presenters' workshops
- publishers' sessions on new materials

3 Organize your time at the conference: look at the conference program and note the sessions and events you're most interested in. One strategy

is to choose as many sessions as you can on a particular topic (e.g. teaching academic writing), so that the conference serves almost as a workshop or seminar on that topic. Some conferences also offer the opportunity to attend a short course. Alternatively, you may want to choose a variety of different sessions on topics that you are not familiar with in order to get a sense of what's new and what's hot in the field. And if you find you are in a session that turns out to not be what you expected, feel free to leave quietly and use your time in some other way. (Sitting near the exit is always a good idea in case you find yourself in this situation.)

4 Network with other participants: find people who have similar interests to you and share a coffee break or meal with them. Don't spend time only with people you already know but try to connect with people who may have interesting things to share with you.

5 Connect with the speakers: presenters are always happy when people are interested in their presentation and are delighted to chat with you after a presentation, and to exchange emails or business cards if you have things you would like to share or discuss as a follow up.

6 Make time for yourself: find time during the day to think about and reflect on the sessions you have attended. You may find it useful to make brief notes about sessions that you found interesting and consider how you can apply what you learned to your own teaching context. These notes will also be helpful if you are later asked to report on your conference participation at your school.

7 Share with colleagues: when you return to your school your colleagues may want to know what you learned from the conference. So share information or videos of some of the sessions over lunch and talk about some of the interesting talks you went to, people you met, and other activities you enjoyed at the conference.

8 Look for opportunities to participate in a future conference: consider if you have a practice, an activity, or relevant experience that could form the basis of a conference presentation; either one you could make on your own, or one that could be a joint presentation with colleagues. This could be a poster session, a paper, workshop, or demonstration.

Develop research skills

Teaching and research go hand in hand, since in every lesson things happen that can be a basis for further understanding. Research simply means collecting information about an issue to better understand it.

27. Learn how to review a textbook
28. Carry out action research
29. Try a replication study
30. Take part in lesson-study

Learn how to review a textboook

Purpose: to develop experience in evaluating textbooks

Many teachers make use of commercial textbooks, and understanding the nature of textbooks is helpful if you are on a team involved in selecting and evaluating materials. In this tip suggestions are given for reviewing a textbook using a set of questions as a guide. This activity can be carried out by a group of teachers or by an individual teacher.

1 Examine the organization of the book by considering these questions:

- Goals. What does the book seek to achieve and how clearly are its learning outcomes identified?
- Syllabus. Is the syllabus adequate or would it need to be supplemented (e.g. through additional activities)?
- Theoretical framework. What language-learning theory is the book based on?
- Methodology. What methodology is the book based on? Is it pedagogically sound?
- Language content. What kind of language does it contain and is it an appropriate level of difficulty for the learners?
- Other content. Are the topics appropriate for the target learners?
- Organization. Is the book well organized into units and lessons, and within lessons are the purposes of activities clearly identified? Do units have a coherent, consistent organization, and do they gradually progress in difficulty throughout the book?
- Activities. Are activities engaging, varied, and useful?
- Teacher appeal. Does the book look easy to teach and is it self-contained, or would the teacher need to develop supplementary materials to use with it?
- Learner appeal. How engaging would it be for learners? How would they rate the design of the book, the topics and the kinds of activities included? Is the material clearly relevant to their perceived language-learning needs? Are self-study components included?

- Ancillaries. What other components does the book include, such as teacher's book, workbook, tests, and digital and web-based support?
- Price. Is the book affordable for the intended buyers?

2 Examine the format of a unit from the textbook: choose one unit from the textbook for closer analysis in order to understand how the content of the unit is organized.

- What are the aims and objectives of the unit?
- What syllabus strands does it contain?
- What is the format or structure of the unit and how is it organized?
- What different kinds of exercises or activities does the unit contain?

3 Experience a textbook-based lesson: teach a unit from the book following the suggestions given in the teacher's book. Following the lesson experience, consider questions such as these:

- What did you like most or least about it?
- What kinds of language use did the unit practice?
- What specific learning outcomes did the material deliver?
- Was there adequate scaffolding of tasks?
- Did you experience any difficulties with any of the activities?
- Would the material work with a mixed-level class?
- How engaging were the activities?

4 Adaptation of the book: consider the suitability of the book in relation to your teaching context and whether some forms of adaptation may be needed.

- Modifying content. Is there content that needs to be modified to better address learners' needs?
- Adding or deleting content. Should anything be added or removed?
- Reorganizing content. Is the sequence of content appropriate, or should some of it be rearranged?

5 Relevance to the teaching context: you can now make a decision on whether you would recommend the course for use in your school.

Richards, J. C. (2015). Materials design in language teacher education: An example from Southeast Asia. In Farrell, T. (ed). *International Perspectives on Language Teacher Education*. Basingstoke: Palgrave Macmillan. 90–106.
Siegel, A. (2014). What should we talk about? The authenticity of textbook topics. *ELT Journal 68(4)*, 363–375.

Carry out action research

28

Purpose: to understand the nature of action research and how to implement it

Action research is teacher-conducted research that seeks to clarify and resolve practical teaching issues and problems. "Research" here refers simply to collecting information. "Action" means that the process involved addresses a classroom issue that you want to explore. This tip clarifies the nature of action research and how to conduct it.

1 Understand the nature of action research: action research has the following features:

- It is built around your normal classroom practice and adds another dimension to practice.
- Its goal is to improve teaching and learning.
- It is small scale and problem-oriented.
- You can carry out action research on your own or with colleagues.
- It views you as a change agent seeking to improve your understanding of teaching through carrying out action research in your own classes.

2 Stages involved in action research:

- Identify an issue you would like to take action on.
- Consider ways of addressing the problem.
- Develop an action plan to try to resolve the issue – the "intervention" – and consider the time and resources needed.
- Implement the plan and observe its effects.
- If necessary, modify the intervention and repeat the process.

3 Choosing a topic for action research: choose a small-scale issue and frame a question that you want to answer. For example:

- How can I help my learners remember new words?
- How can I reduce the amount of talking I do during my lessons?
- How can I deal with a mixed-level speaking class?

4 Choosing a strategy to address the problem: select a way to address the problem that will bring about a change of some kind.

5 Choosing a way of evaluating the results: decide on a way to evaluate the impact of the change. For example:

- a questionnaire to students
- a survey
- a video record of a lesson
- a test or other form of assessment.

6 An example of action research:

> *Recently, I wanted to find out if peer feedback in my composition class helps improve my learners' writing, and decided to try out action research. I first had to develop a procedure for carrying out peer feedback, guidelines for my students to follow and a checklist that they can make use of. I also gave several practice sessions to demonstrate how the process works. Then we used peer feedback as an alternative to teacher feedback on my students' compositions throughout a semester-long composition class and kept notes on how it works. At the end of the course, I surveyed my students' opinions about peer feedback, and compared their writing to see if it had improved. My conclusion was that it has made a difference to my students' writing. However, I needed to make some changes to the checklist I had developed and will try it again with another class next semester.*

(Jose, institute teacher, Ecuador)

Can you identify the stages involved in action research from this example, as outlined in part 2 above?

7 Recommendations:

- In addressing the problem, choose strategies that relate to or reflect your usual classroom practices.
- Consider working with a colleague, for example, two teachers could use the same intervention strategy and compare the results.
- Give careful consideration to the amount of time involved.
- If you find your action research made a difference, share your findings with other teachers.

Burns, A. (1999). *Collaborative Action Research for English Language Teachers.* Cambridge: Cambridge University Press.
Wyatt, M. (2010) Teachers researching their own practice. *ELT Journal* 65(4), 417–425.

Try a replication study

29

Purpose: to learn techniques that can be used to study your own classroom

In order to better understand the nature of teaching and learning, it is helpful to explore questions about these processes and to collect information about how they take place. This tip considers the value of repeating a piece of research that has been carried out in a different context to see whether what was discovered is also true in your own setting.

1 Nature of replication research: replication research means repeating a study using the same procedures, but in a different setting and with different subjects. For example, you may read an article that reports on how teachers use questions and the kinds of questions they most often use with adults. You decide to repeat the study to see if you get the same results when you collect information about your own use of questions in your adult classes.

2 Benefits of replicating someone else's study: replication research can have several purposes for teachers:

- It enables you to see if the research findings apply to your situation.
- It enables you to learn about the process of conducting research.
- It adds the role of "teacher-researcher" to your role.

3 Choosing a study to replicate: a number of factors need to be considered in choosing a study to replicate:

- The research raises questions that are relevant to your situation.
- It is manageable in terms of time and resources you have available.
- It does not require the use of procedures that you may not be familiar with (such as statistical analysis of information).

Professional ESL teacher journals often contain example of issues that could be a focus of a follow-up study. For example, recent issues of *ELT Journal* included reports on research on the following topics:

- the kind of feedback supervisors gave to teachers after observation
- the ways in which teachers explained vocabulary in reading classes
- the kinds of changes students made when they revised compositions.

4 An example: the following is an example of the kind of project that could easily be replicated (from Richards and Lockhart, 1994):

- A group of teachers in an institute were interested in the kind of feedback they gave to their learners on their spoken errors.
- They videotaped lessons of classes with different levels.
- They reviewed the videos and focused on the errors students made, and noted the ones that the teachers corrected and how they corrected them.
- They found that in the beginning level, students were generally corrected because they were not understood. The amount of error-correction depended on the level of the class. In the upper-intermediate classes, 80 percent of errors were ignored, while in the beginning and intermediate classes, only 30 percent of errors were ignored. They also found that they corrected fewer errors in open-ended communication activities or unguided discussion. They found that the usual way that errors were corrected was to interrupt the learner and ask them to repeat the correct form.
- On discussing the findings, the teachers felt that the types of errors they corrected was appropriate, but that a greater variety of error-correction strategies could be made use of.

A piece of research of this kind is an ideal topic for a follow-up study for several reasons:

- It can be done individually or as a group project.
- It addresses a topic that all teachers are interested in.
- The research procedures are relatively straightforward.
- It generates information that can be applied to classroom practice.
- It would make a good topic for a presentation.

Richards, J. C. & Lockhart, C. (1994). *Reflective Teaching in Second Language Classrooms* (pp. 200–201). New York: Cambridge University Press.
Wyatt, M. (2011). Teachers researching their own practice. *ELT Journal 65(4)*, 417–425.

Take part in lesson-study

30

> **Purpose: to learn through engaging in shared lesson-planning**

Lesson-study refers to a process in which a group of teachers co-plan a lesson that focuses on addressing a particular problem or issue. One of the teachers later teaches the lesson, and then the group meets to review and reflect on their experience. Through working together with other teachers, participants have a chance to learn from each other and to share and compare their understandings of teaching. It is an approach which focuses on solving issues that you identify in your own practice, and enables you to develop strategies that you can apply in your classes. This tip describes how to implement lesson-study as a professional development activity.

1 Preparing for lesson-study: a workshop can provide a good introduction to the lesson-study approach. Once you are familiar with the approach, you can choose how often you would like to take part in it, and how easily you can arrange to work as a group and carry out the observation phase of the project.

2 Forming a group: like other group-based activities, a small group of three to six teachers is a good size for a lesson-study project. Sometimes it is useful for the group to consist of teachers with different levels of experience so that inexperienced teachers can learn how more experienced teachers think and act. At other times, a group may consist of expert teachers who wish to try out novel and creative ways of teaching.

3 Identify a goal: the primary goal of lesson-study is to develop an effective way of improving student learning, often as a response to a problem or issue that your group has identified. The members of the group share ideas on possible issues or problems you could explore through lesson-study. The following are examples of topics that could be the focus of lesson-study:

- How can we use texts to teach critical reading?
- How can we teach grammar in a more communicative way?
- How can we teaching reading as an interactive process?
- What's an effective way of building a lesson around a recorded lecture?
- What are some strategies for differentiated instruction in a writing class?

In choosing a goal for a project, you need to consider what the students should be able to do at the end of a lesson designed to address the issue you have identified, i.e. you should identify one or more learning outcomes that you want a lesson to achieve.

4 Plan a lesson: your group then plans a lesson to address the question or problem you have identified. As you plan the lesson, discuss what your expectations are for the lesson, how you think it will promote students' learning, and what the expected outcomes of the lesson are.

5 Teach the lesson: one of the group volunteers to teach the lesson to their class. The other group members observe the lesson and take notes or collect information on the effectiveness of the lesson and what the learners learned from it. The observation phase of lesson-study is a crucial part of the process, since it requires careful attention to trying to identify how students are learning, how much they are learning, and whether what you observe reflects your expectations as to how the lesson would work.

6 Reflect and revise: your group then reflects on the lesson and discusses whether the lesson achieved its goals and if it needs to be revised or improved. Once changes to the lesson plan are made, a second teacher agrees to teach the lesson while the other group members observe.

7 Share: your group shares what you have learned with other colleagues.

Fernandez, C. (2002). Learning from Japanese approaches to professional development: The case of lesson-study. *Journal of Teacher Education*, 53(5), 393–405.

Expand your teaching skills

We often tend to make use of a set of tried and tested teaching techniques and strategies. It is also important to sometimes move beyond our comfort zone and try doing things differently.

31. Experience classroom activities
32. Watch videos of teaching
33. Use wikis for collaborative teacher development
34. Take part in micro-teaching
35. Be creative

31 Experience classroom activities

Purpose: to learn how activities work through experiencing them as learners

After some years as a teacher, we tend make use of a core of tried and tested activities that work well for the kind of students we teach. Most often, I find that we tend to view these activities from the point of view of the teacher. This tip focuses on how we can understand the nature and value of a classroom activity by assuming the role of a learner and participating in or completing an activity or task in the way a learner would normally do: a process sometimes referred to as *loop input*.

1 Understand the nature of the process: this tip requires you – either individually or working with other teachers – to design an activity or task of the kind you use with your learners, to carry out the activity in the role of a learner, and then to reflect on what can be learned from it.

2 Choose an activity to explore: you may either to decide to experience an activity from your regular repertoire of teaching techniques, or to experience an unfamiliar activity in order to learn more about it.

3 An example of how the process works: we will use, as an example, a reading activity known as *reciprocal reading*, an activity that can be used in a reading class. The basis for this approach is that the students take much of the responsibility for teaching. The students become the teacher in small-group reading sessions. They are assigned a text to read and then both the teacher and the students share a discussion about the meaning of the text. Four strategies are used to guide the discussion: *predicting, question-generating, summarizing,* and *clarifying.*

4 A typical reciprocal reading lesson follows these stages:

A text has been chosen as the basis for the reading lesson. The text has been divided into its major sections. The class is divided into small groups. One member of each group is nominated as the "teacher" of the group. Their role is to guide the group members as they read the text.

The teacher normally models the four strategies the students are asked to apply by demonstrating the use of each strategy when reading the first section of the text:

- Predicting. The students are asked to predict what the text might be about.
- Questioning. Students generate questions as they read. These may be of different kinds, such as literal, inferential, or critical thought questions.
- Summarizing. In pairs, students verbally summarize, then share their summary with the group.
- Clarifying. Students raise any queries related to words, phrases, or anything in the text that they did not understand.

5 Experience reciprocal reading from the viewpoint of learners: if possible, run the activity with a group of interested colleagues. Choose a relatively challenging article of interest as the basis for the activity. This could be on any topic that might be of interest to you. (Preview the article to decide how it can be divided into sections if the article is not already made up of clearly identifiable sections.) Read the article, following the four stages suggested as a basis for reciprocal reading: predicting, questioning, summarizing, clarifying.

Following the activity, review the experience, and reflect on how it worked, how well, and how useful it could be in teaching your students. Questions you could consider include:

- What kind of students would benefit from this activity?
- What problems might arise in using it?
- What are its advantages or disadvantages as a regular class activity?
- How does it compare with other kinds of reading activities?

6 Other activities to try out in this way: many other familiar classroom routines can also be tried out in a similar way, such as, e.g. dictogloss, role play, or minimal pairs. If possible, do the activity in a shared second language.

Woodwood, T. (1988). *Loop input*. Canterbury: Pilgrims.
DelliCarpini, M. (2009). Enhancing cooperative learning in Tesol teacher education. *ELT Journal 63(1)*, 42–50.

32

Watch videos of teaching

Purpose: watch videos to see how teachers deliver their lessons and explore different aspects of teaching

A video recording of a lesson provides a rich source of information for examining different aspects of teaching. Depending on the type of lesson that is viewed, video can be used to explore many different dimensions of lessons, focusing either on the teacher, the students, or both. In this tip, we focus on how watching videos of lessons, either individually or in a group, can be used to explore different perspectives on teaching.

1 Sources of videos: there are examples of many different kinds of lessons available on the internet and these have the advantage of being "anonymous" since they are not lessons of teachers that you know.

2 The context of the lesson: it is important to understand the context of the lesson where possible, such as the school, the class, the teacher, the learners, and the teacher's goal for the lesson. When available, the teacher's lesson plan should also be provided. Often times, teachers are willing to provide a video of one or more lessons. If this is the case, it is important to emphasize that the videos are not used to evaluate the lesson, but to serve as a source of reflection and learning.

3 The goals of watching the video: depending on your interests and purposes, goals such as the following may be chosen:

How does the teacher:

- introduce the lesson, tasks and activities
- group students
- monitor student performance
- arouse students' interest in the lesson or an activity
- ask and answer questions
- deal with classroom management
- give learners feedback?

If you are working in a group, different members can focus on one or two items from such a list. Following the viewing, reflect on your observations. You may focus on questions such as these:

- Did you notice anything that particularly impressed you?
- Would you have used the same lesson procedures?
- What would you have done differently, and why?

4 Observing in different roles: sometimes it is useful to observe a lesson from the point of view of a supervisor, a teacher or a student. In this case, different viewing purposes can be identified for those in each role.

For supervisors

- How clear were the teacher's instructions?
- How well-sequenced were the activities?
- How effective was the teacher's use of class time?
- How well-paced was the lesson?
- Did the teacher succeed in engaging all of the students in the lesson?

For teachers

- What aspects of the lesson went well?
- Were there any aspects that did not go so well?
- What challenges arose during the lesson?
- How satisfied were you with the lesson?

For students

- How engaging were the activities used?
- Did you find the activities too easy or too difficult?
- What did you learn during the lesson?
- What is the most important thing you will take away from the lesson?

Following the viewing, group members can role-play a conversation between the supervisor and the teacher, and a student and the teacher.

5 Finally, reflect on what you have learned from watching the video and from the role-play activities, where appropriate.

Gun, B. (2011). Quality self-reflection through reflection training. *ELT Journal 65(2)*, 126–135.
Eroz-Tuga, B. (2013). Reflective feedback sessions using video recordings. *ELT Journal 67(2)*, 175–183.

33

Use wikis for collaborative teacher development

Purpose: to understand how to use wikis to interact with other teachers

A wiki is a collaborative website that allows users to collect, organize, create, and revise content. They are widely used in education, providing a forum for teachers and students to interact between and among themselves, supporting both student learning and collaborative teacher development. This tip describes how wikis function and how they can be used for professional development.

1 Purposes: while wikis have many uses in education, for language teachers they provide a way for us to share and develop knowledge related to teaching issues, allowing us to support each other's teaching and professional development. They may contain hyperlinks to videos, materials, and other items, and can be used to help find group solutions to a problem, to discuss common questions and concerns, and to provide a source for sharing teaching tips and activities. They also help teachers become part of a professional learning community and can serve as a follow-up to other forms of professional development, providing a forum for discussion, materials development, and reflection.

2 Joining a wiki community: use a search engine to find wiki communities in your particular field of interest, e.g. ESP, EAP. When you enter a wiki, you are able to read what the wiki's community has written. Clicking on the "edit" button on an article enables you to edit and add to the article's text. Edits made by members of the community are stored in a revision history, together with the author of the revision.

3 Starting a wiki community: guidance on creating a wiki is given at Wikispaces home page (choose "Teachers"). To build a wiki community, a number of factors should be kept in mind:

- Have a clear goal for the wiki.
- Be clear about who your intended audience is.
- Make sure that there is a moderator or editor to review submissions to make sure they are relevant and useful.
- Provide clear instructions on how to contribute to the wiki.

Here is an example from a wiki group applying the Dogme approach.

Phil
Hi
I'm a new Dogme member and I've been experimenting with Dogme in my classes.
I've been doing materials free discussions followed by language focus, work and practice. ....
Am I doing the dogme bit right?
Cheers

Rob
Hi Phil,
Thank you for sharing this classroom experience. I feel uncomfortable telling you whether you are doing Dogme "right", but I can say a materials-free discussion followed by learners generating notes for themselves seems dogmetic indeed....Regards,
Rob (USA)

Phil
...My only concerns are the language focus bits. 8 am on a Monday morning may not be my best time to think grammatically on my toes... So, how would you advise I approach the language focus and also grammar/ language input?

Dennis
Phil
I don't want to sound like a cranky missionary, but since you ask for comments and suggestions vis-a-vis grammar I can't help urging the point of view that it is not "grammar" itself that needs covering or studying or learning but being able to say, mean what you want to mean and using the resources of English as efficiently as possible to do so....

Phil
Thanks to all your comments and tips I've managed to survive and quite enjoy a Dogmeticish (??) week. It is the first time I've seen students actually interested and giving their own true opinions. ...

As the example above suggests, Wikis provide an opportunity for teachers to take part in meaningful collaborative learning, they can foster the development of a virtual community of practice, and they allow teachers to benefit from their shared experience, and expertise.

Using Wikispaces to facilitate teaching and learning:
http://www.tesl-ej.org/wordpress/issues/volume16/ej62/ej62m2/
Chatfield, T. B. (2009). *The Complete Guide to Wikis: How to Set Up, Use, and Benefit from Wikis for Teachers, Business Professionals, Families, and Friends.* Atlantic Publishing Group Inc.

34

Take part in micro-teaching

> **Purpose: to practice and develop teaching skills through micro-teaching**

Micro-teaching involves a teacher planning and teaching a short lesson to a group of fellow teachers (or to ESOL students who have volunteered to serve as student teachers in a micro-teaching class). Micro-teaching is based on the view that a complex skill such as teaching can be broken down into its individual components, and these can be practiced one at a time until the complexity of teaching has been mastered. This tip explains how micro-teaching can be used as a teacher development activity.

1 Procedure: micro-teaching is usually based on a sequence of *plan*, *teach*, and *critique*, and has three essential features:

- The teacher plans and teachers a micro-lesson of five to ten minutes.
- The lesson has a very specific and narrow focus.
- It is immediately followed by a critique of the teacher's performance.

2 Understanding the goals of micro-teaching: micro-teaching is often used as a training procedure for novice teachers. However, the micro-teaching format can also be used as a teacher-development activity for other teachers. In this case, it has a different goal and makes use of procedures that depend on reflection and discussion, rather than critiquing the teacher's performance. It can be a useful strategy when a new set of teaching materials is being introduced; to try out tasks and activities; or when teachers wish to address a problem or issue that they are experiencing with some aspect of their teaching.

3 Planning a micro-teaching activity: this is a group process in which teachers work together and take turns teaching a micro-lesson to the group, following which they discuss and reflect on their experience of the lesson. This activity works best if there is a group of six or more teachers.

4 Length of the lesson: by definition micro-lessons are usually relatively short, but it depends on the kind of lesson it is. They could be as short as five minutes but could also be 15 to 20 minutes in length.

5 Focus on a micro-lesson: for the purposes of micro-teaching the lesson consists of an activity rather than a complete lesson. The lesson should focus on something that can be presented as an uninterrupted sequence, as it normally would be in class. During an initial planning meeting the group chooses activities that will be used for the purpose of micro-lessons. Examples of things of this kind are:

- an unfamiliar exercise type in a textbook
- one part of a cycle in a communicative, text-based, or task-based lesson
- one part of the sequence of activities in a process-writing lesson
- a deductive activity in a grammar lesson
- a problem-solving task
- a discussion activity
- use of whiteboard software
- developing grammatical awareness from a reading text
- effective use of realia in a speaking class.

6 The micro-lesson sequence: one of the members of the group offers to play the part of teacher and the other members of the group play the role of students as the "teacher" presents the lesson. In some cases, one of the group members can act as an observer and take notes on any points of interest that are observed during the lesson.

7 Following the lesson: the "teacher" first explains their reasons for the lesson they taught, mentions any difficulties that were encountered in planning the lesson, and discusses the rationale for how the lesson was presented. The other group members then share their experience of the lesson, what they think worked well, anything that did not work so well, and whether they would teach the lesson or the activity in the same way in their classes.

The group then reflects on how useful they found the micro-teaching experience and suggests any improvements or changes they might incorporate in subsequent micro-lessons.

35 Be creative

> **Purpose: to learn creative strategies for designing activities**

One of the things that experience brings to teaching is the knowledge of how to conduct our lessons fluently, drawing on well-established procedures and activities. However, one consequence of this is that we may draw on the same strategies and techniques and rarely add new ones to our repertoire. The focus of this tip is on developing new ways of teaching through the use of creative materials and activities.

1 Understanding creativity: creativity involves the ability to solve problems in original and valuable ways that are relevant to goals; to see new meanings and relationships in things and make connections; to have original thoughts and ideas about something; to use the imagination and past experience to create new learning possibilities.

Look at some ways of practicing the past tense. Rank them from most (1) to least (5) creative. Can you add two creative ideas of your own?

- Charades. Students act out or mime an activity – others describe what they did using the past tense.
- A milestone. Students write about or discuss a milestone in their life and the events that led up it.
- Stories. Students are given phrases to start a story. Each member of a group develops the story by adding a sentence in the past tense.
- News photos. Students are given a news picture and have to make up a story to go with it.

2 Benefits of creativity: what benefits does creative teaching bring to a) the teacher b) the learners c) the school?

3 Test your creativity: try this task then compare your thoughts with a colleague, if possible. How creative were you?

A teacher has just called in sick. You are going to teach her 50-minute spoken English class, lower-intermediate level, in five minutes. Your only teaching aid is an empty glass. Describe your lesson plan.

4 Developing creative tasks: the following aspects of task design can lead to creative tasks (Dörnyei, 2001). Review the list and examine a textbook. Can you find examples of activities with some of these features?

- *Challenge*: tasks in which learners solve problems, discover something, overcome obstacles, or find information.
- *Interesting content*: topics that students are likely to find interesting and that they would want to read about outside of class.
- *The personal element*: activities that make connections to the learners' lives and concerns.
- *The novelty element*: aspects of an activity that are new or different or totally unexpected.
- *The intriguing element*: tasks that concern ambiguous, problematic, paradoxical, controversial, contradictory or incongruous material and that stimulate curiosity.
- *Individual choice*: tasks that give students a personal choice and that require a personal response.
- *Encourage risk-taking*: tasks that require students to go beyond what they are comfortable with.
- *Original thought*: activities that require a creative response.
- *The fantasy element*: activities that engage the learners' fantasy and that invite the learners to use their imagination for creating make-believe stories, identifying with fictional characters or acting out imaginary situations.

5 Adapting tasks: did you find activities in the book you examined that could be made more creative? Choose three and suggest ways in which they could be adapted.

6 Developing creative tasks: choose content that could form the basis of a lesson or activity for a specific teaching context. This could be a) a print text b) a video clip c) an aspect of grammar d) a text-type such as a narrative or piece of descriptive writing. Discuss ways of building creative elements into the design of exercise and activities. Then compare your ideas with others.

7 Creativity in the school: schools can encourage creativity by helping teachers recognize and share what is creative in their own practice. Suggest three ways in which creativity can be encouraged in your school.

Dörnyei, Z. (2001). *Motivational Strategies in the Language Classroom*. Cambridge: Cambridge University Press.

Tin, T. B. (2013). Towards creativity in ELT: the need to say something new. *ELT Journal* 67(4), 385–397.

Research your own teaching

There are several simple techniques that can be used for collecting information about your own teaching. Through classroom research you can better understand both how you teach and how your learners learn.

---

36. Use narrative frames to explore teaching
37. Use narrative writing
38. Monitor your teacher talking time (TTT)
39. Monitor your action zone
40. Use a case study to explore teaching and learning

Use narrative frames to explore teaching

Purpose: to learn through sharing stories about teaching

Often when we talk about teaching with our colleagues we tell stories: we talk about things that happened, giving information about where we were, what we did, what happened next, and so on. Stories are a great way of sharing experience, since when I tell a story, you will often share your story of a similar experience. Some of my most memorable encounters with teachers began with a teacher telling me a story about something unusual, interesting, insightful, or challenging that occurred in one of their classes. In this tip we consider narrative frames as a way of describing and reflecting on teaching incidents.

1 What is a narrative frame? As its name suggests, a narrative frame is essentially a partial skeleton of a story. It provides some of the elements of the story, and the reader completes the story with his or her own information. The frame serves to focus the story on key elements, and serves as a source of information that can be reviewed and discussed with other teachers. It is an approach that can be used to foster critical reflection.

2 Examples of a narrative frame: complete these narrative frames with your own information. You might like to compare your responses with a colleague, if possible.

My first year teaching English
1. The first English class I ever taught was in _____ . The class I was teaching was _____
2. At first I found teaching to be _____
3. Once I got used to it however _____
4. The most difficult part of teaching for me was _____
5. I found the best way to deal with this was to _____
6. The first book I taught from was called _____
7. The thing I remember most about the book is _____
8. One of my happiest memories from that time is _____
9. The thing I learned most in my first year of teaching was _____
10. The advice I would give to someone who is starting out in teaching would be _____ _____

A critical incident

This frame focuses on a critical incident relating to a problem that you encountered recently in teaching one of your classes.

1. Recently I was teaching a class of _____ .
2. The goal of the lesson was _____ .
3. The materials I was using were _____ .
4. The students in this class are usually _____ .
5. At one point in the lesson I needed to change direction a little because _____ .
6. I thought about possible responses and then I decided to _____ .
7. As a result of my decision _____ .
8. When I look back on what I did I feel _____ .

3 Using narratives frames as a group activity: here are some suggestions on how to use narrative frames as the basis of a group activity.

When using narrative frames in teachers' groups, teachers take turns preparing frames on topics of interest. For example, topics could include:

- how you made best use of an assigned textbook
- experiences in using group work
- recollections of an exceptional teacher
- experiences in trying to learn a new language
- dealing with disruptive students in a class.

Up to ten or more sentence starters are then developed which, when completed, will form a narrative, as with the examples above.

The sentence starters are distributed in advance of a group meeting. Group members complete the frames with their own information. When the group meets, the completed frames are compared and responded to. Through follow-up questions and discussion, the group examines the meaning of the story and considers its implications for teaching practice.

Burkhuizen, G. & Wette, R. (2008). Narrative frames for exploring the experiences of language teachers. *System 36(3)*, 327–387.

Purpose: to use narrative writing to find new meanings in teaching

Some of the most powerful accounts of teaching have come from narratives written by people who are not language teachers, such as Sylvia Ashton Warner's *Teacher*, or Frank McCourt's *Teacher man*. When we frame an experience as a narrative, we can use it both to record an event but also to trigger new ideas and understandings. The process of writing about a teaching incident can sometimes serve to reveal or clarify things we may not have been aware of. In this tip we examine the use of narrative writing as a way of exploring and reflecting on teaching.

1 The nature of narrative writing: narratives are the retellings of past experiences framed in terms of a setting, characters, incidents, and a conclusion. In this tip we use narrative writing as it applies to short, written accounts of teaching incidents or events.

2 The purpose of narrative writing: like other forms of written responses to teaching moments, narrative writing serves both as an account of events and an attempt to find the meaning of the events.

3 The focus of narrative writing: the focus of narrative writing is descriptions of different kinds of experiences. These could include:

- accounts of dilemmas or problems
- accounts of insights that arise during teaching
- responses to classroom incidents
- classroom activities and how they were used
- reflections on language learning.

4 Example of a narrative: the following narrative describes an insight a teacher in the UAE arrived at while teaching:

The longer I teach the more often "teachable moments" emerge in my teaching. It might be a topic, a particular text, a situation – many prompts can invite me to share a story or an experience with my learners which relates to the lesson goals. Usually, I find these diversions are helpful; sometimes they relieve tension when we have been working hard on something.

For instance, one day I was working through some examples with my EAP class of how to integrate another writer's ideas into my own text. In the example I was using, one of the learners suddenly stopped me to ask about the name of one of the authors in the in-text citation. Since I had noticed that my learners frequently confused Western authors' first and family names, this gave me a perfect opportunity to draw attention to the names of the authors in the text and to ask them to suggest what the citation would be if each of them had written the original text. Personalizing the example in this way and being willing to be diverted from the focus of the activity at hand is sometimes necessary. I usually tell myself if one learner has thought it important enough to ask the question, others are likely to be wondering about the same thing. It's important to be ready to let the learners' agenda take over at times.

(Sara Cotterall)

4 The audience for narrative writing: there are two kinds of audiences. One is you as a writer; the other audience could be your colleagues. You can invite them to pose questions or responses to a narrative and then use these to initiate conversation and discussion.

5 The format for narrative writing:

- Start with a clear description of the context or situation. Give some background information.
- Describe the incident or events that prompted you to write.
- Give your reflection or response to the incident. The response may also include questions that require further thought or reflection.

6 Assembling narratives: narratives may be used in several ways: as a component of a portfolio or journal; as a stand-alone collection for reflection; for use as a basis for discussion in a teacher learning group (see Tip 20).

Monitor your teacher talking time (TTT)

Purpose: to observe the amount of teacher talk in lessons

Effective lessons are very much dependent on how the teacher guides the processes of teaching and learning. Much of this guidance happens through teacher talk – as the teacher scaffolds learning, models language use, and checks students' understanding. A challenge for us as teachers is to provide rather than minimize opportunities for student participation. Sometimes however, there is too much teacher talk (*Teacher Talk Time* or *TTT*) in lessons because the lesson is dominated by the teacher. In fact, in some lessons I observe, individual students may only speak for two or three minutes during the entire lesson. This tip focuses on monitoring the amount of teacher talk that you use during a lesson. This requires you to either audio record one or more of your lessons, or to invite a colleague to observe your class and to monitor how much time the students were speaking during the lesson.

1 Why so much teacher talk? The following are some reasons why teachers sometimes talk a lot during lessons. Can you add others?

- They need to manage and control the lesson.
- They want to make sure students understand.
- They want to provide the students with models of good English.
- The students expect it.
- The students prefer the teacher to talk rather than speak themselves.

2 Finding out how much teacher talk you use in lessons: audio-record your lesson or ask a colleague to use a lesson observation form. As you listen to the recording of your lesson, note in minutes the amount of time you talk during the lesson. As your colleague observes your lesson, they should record how much you talk and how much the learners talk.

3 What was the amount of teacher talk in the lesson as a percentage of the available lesson time?

4 If you audio-recorded your lesson, listen to the recording again. Note in minutes each time the following occurs:

- social talk
- giving instructions
- answering questions
- giving feedback
- other.

5 Reducing the amount of teacher talk in a lesson: if you find that your teacher talking time takes up too much of the lesson, consider the following questions and identify some ways in which you could increase the amount of student talking time in lessons:

1) Did you spend too long on some parts of the lesson? How could you have used the time more effectively?
2) Were you taking too long to explain the lesson's goals or to introduce and clarify a task or activity? If so, what are some ways in which you could take less time to communicate the same information?
3) Did you spend time reviewing homework or checking answers? Could some of these things be done by the learners themselves?
4) Did you ask too many questions during the lesson? Were all of the questions necessary?
5) Did you take too long to answer students' questions? Could some of their questions have been answered by other members of the class?
6) Did you spend too long explaining the meaning of words or grammar items? Could students find some of the answers themselves working in pairs or groups?
7) Did you give students enough time to complete activities or to answer questions? Did you encourage them to discuss activities in English as they carried them out?
8) Did you spend most of the class time standing in front of the class talking? Could you have made greater use of pair-work and group-work activities?

6 Try out the strategies you identified and monitor one or more of your lessons again to find out if you have been able to reduce your TTT.

Dellar, H. (2004). Rethinking Teacher Talking Time. *TESOL Spain Newsletter*.
http://www.tesol-spain.org/newsletter/hughdellar.html
Lynch, T. (1996). *Communication in the Language Classroom*. Oxford: Oxford University Press.
Scrivener, J. (2005). *Learning Teaching* (2nd Ed.). Macmillan.

Purpose: to observe your pattern of interaction with students in your class

An important dimension of teaching is the extent to which the teacher engages with all the students in the class, and not simply those who are most talkative or who are seated near the front of the class. We unconsciously tend to interact more with some students than with others, and the interaction pattern that we typically make use of is known as the teacher's action zone. This tip seeks to identify your typical action zone.

1 Engagement with students: when you teach, do you feel that you usually engage equally with all of the students in the class? How do you usually try to do so? Check the strategies you use below.

- I keep the class list in front of me and am systematic in how I call on students when I ask questions.
- I rearrange the class seating (e.g. in a circle) to provide more opportunities for interaction.
- I learn students' names so I can call on every student.
- I use gesture and eye contact to make contact with students.
- I monitor who has asked or answered a question to make sure some students are not dominating the interaction.
- I change students' seating regularly so the same students are not always at the front or back of the class.
- I teach lessons from different places, e.g. not always from the front of the class.
- I ask students to take turns when they ask questions and not to ask a second question until all of the other students have asked a question.

You might like to compare your responses with those of a colleague or in a group, if possible.

2 Out of the action zone: do you sometimes have students who avoid being in the teacher's action zone because they don't want to be called on? Is this always a bad thing? If you want to change this behavior, how would you go about it?

3 Review of a lesson: now use a recording of a lesson or invite a colleague to observe one or more of your lessons. Using a seating plan for the class, you or an observer can check each time you interact with each member of the class. You can also ask students to keep a tally of how often they were called upon during a lesson, and collect their tally of scores at the end of a lesson.

4 Reflection on the lesson: review the information you obtained about your lesson. Did your lesson reflect an inclusive action zone? If not, what do you think was the reason? Consider the information below:

- Some students were too shy to ask questions.
- Some students' limited English prevented them from interacting.
- I looked more to one side of the class than to the other.
- Some students tend to "disappear" during lessons.
- The age of the students influenced who I interacted with.
- The gender of the students influenced who I interacted with.
- I tended to interact with the more outgoing students.
- I interacted with the students whose names I could remember.
- I couldn't move around very easily because of the arrangement of the desks.

If you feel you need to change your action zone, list three ways in which you could do so. Then try your ideas out over the next few lessons you teach.

Wajnryb, R. (1992). *Classroom Observation Tasks: A Resource Book for Language Teachers and Trainers*. Cambridge: Cambridge University Press.
Richards, J. C. (2015). *Key Issues in Language Teaching*. Cambridge: Cambridge University Press.

Use a case study to explore teaching and learning

Purpose: to understand a situation by collecting information about it over a period of time

A case study involves collecting information about a learner or an activity over a period of time in order to understand an issue more fully, to find out more about learners, and to document aspects of teaching and learning. Since it typically focuses on one situation, it does not generate information or knowledge that can be generalized; however, the information obtained is generally richer and more extensive than information that may obtained in other ways. This tip shows how to conduct a case study and what can be learned from it.

1 Choosing a topic for a case study: as noted above, a case study should seek to explore a topic or issue in depth. Begin by thinking of questions you would like to explore. These might be related to you as a teacher, to your students, or to other aspects of your teaching context. For example:

- How does a teacher adapt a coursebook when using it as the basis for a course?
- What kind of technology does a student make use of to support their language development?
- How does a student make use of feedback on their writing?
- What do students learn from watching television?

2 Collecting information in a case study: there are different ways information can be collected for a case study. For example, for the suggestions above you could:

- look at the lesson plans the teacher used when teaching from the book
- ask the student to complete a checklist every week for a time period
- monitor the corrections the student makes to his or her work during a semester
- ask a student to keep a learning log over a month and to note daily new words or expressions they learned.

3 Example of a case study:

Teachers in an EAP program wanted to explore the learners' needs for English and the situations that were most problematic for the students. Four of the teachers decided to monitor one student each over the period of one semester, choosing students from different academic departments. Each teacher worked with one student and asked each student to keep a daily record of situations where they needed to use English and any difficulties they encountered. For this the students were asked to use a checklist that the teachers had prepared.

Once a week, the teachers met the student they were monitoring and discussed the reports the students had made. During these conversations the teacher discussed strategies each student made use of to cope with difficult situations and the teacher also gave their own suggestions.

At the end of the semester, the four teachers got together to review and compare the information they had about each student. During their discussion they focused on questions such as:

- Were the experiences of each student typical or unusual in any way?
- What surprising or unexpected information did the students describe?
- Were there any patterns or similarities in their experiences?
- How useful did the students find the case study experience?
- How useful did the teachers find it?
- Would a follow-up involving a larger sample of students be useful, perhaps using a questionnaire or survey?
- Were there any findings from the case studies that could be applied to the design of the courses for international students?

For a famous case study, see the reference at the bottom of the page.

Schmidt, R. (1983). Interaction, acculturation and the acquisition of communicative competence. In Wolfson, N. & Judd, E. (eds). *Sociolinguistics and language acquisition.* (pp. 137–174). Rolwey, MA: Newbury House.

Create an institutional professional development culture

Professional development requires the support of the school or institution. It requires opportunities for teachers to work together to help achieve the best results for the school and for those who work and learn within it.

41. Create a culture of teacher development
42. Make the most of meetings
43. Plan a workshop
44. Start a suggestion box

41 Create a culture of teacher development

Purpose: to develop support for teacher development within a school

When I visit schools and teaching institutions, I can often sense fairly quickly whether it is a place where teachers collaborate and work together and where the administration supports teachers and encourages them in teacher development. An institution that believes in the value of professional development expresses confidence in its teachers, encourages adaptation and innovation, is open to new ideas, and supports, encourages, and rewards teachers for pursuing professional development. In this tip we will consider ways in which a culture of professional development can be encouraged.

1 Establish institutional goals for professional development: in order to develop a culture of professional development in a school, the starting point is for administrators and teachers to use group meetings, discussion, and conversation to discuss questions such:

- What is the role of professional development in the institution? Is professional development a responsibility both of the institution as well as the individual?
- How can professional development benefit the institution? In what ways will it improve the performance of the school, and help achieve better learning outcomes?
- How can professional development provide career development for teachers? How can it help teachers advance to more senior positions (e.g. as co-ordinator or curriculum designer) and how will they benefit by acquiring new knowledge and skills? How can it increase job satisfaction and lead to better teacher performance?
- How can professional development support better student learning?

The outcome of the discussions is a document that can be shared among staff in the school for their reactions and suggestions. The result is a position-paper on professional development that everyone agrees on.

2 Find out what the professional development needs of teachers are: the next step involves identifying the current needs of the teachers in the institution. This can be the focus of a group discussion in which the following kinds of issues are discussed, resulting in a document that lists needs related to each area:

- Instructional strengths. What kinds and levels of expertise are represented in the school?
- Communication. What processes are in place to enable teachers to develop cohesive and professional relationships as well as collegiality, and to identify potential for change and improvement?
- Awareness. How are staff encouraged to become aware of research and innovations that could support in-house school development?
- Innovation. Are processes in place to support creative teaching?
- Partnerships. Are opportunities provided for teachers to get support and encouragement from peers through such activities as team teaching, peer observation and shared lesson planning?
- Support. What levels of support exist to encourage teachers to pursue professional development? Do teachers have adequate resources to support their teaching?
- Recognition. Are the skills and expertise of teachers recognized, and are teachers encouraged to share their approaches to and experiences of teacher development? A school can acknowledge the value of professional development by recognizing teachers' efforts in different ways. For example:
  - by acknowledging their achievements in in-house newsletters or annual reports when appropriate
  - by giving them opportunities to mentor novice teachers
  - by encouraging them to share their ideas with others by giving seminars or workshops, or leading a discussion in meetings.

3 Produce a professional development plan for both the institution and for individual teachers: a useful activity for a workshop or school review activity is for teachers and administrators to draw up a plan that includes short-term and longer-term goals for both the institution and for teachers, and to consider the steps that are needed to realize the plan.

Make the most of meetings

Purpose: to consider a constructive role for meetings as a form of professional development

Meetings serve a variety of purposes in schools and other institutions, and often serve little purpose except as means of communicating information from the administration. However, meetings can serve a more useful role. When I was head of a large university department, I found that many of the problems teachers raised could be resolved more effectively when they were discussed within the format of a meeting, allowing other colleagues to come up with suggestions and solutions. In this tip we consider a productive role for meetings as a means of fostering professional development.

1 Purposes of meetings: apart from opportunities to transmit information, meetings can also serve other purposes. How often do meetings serve the purposes below in your experience? Do they sometimes serve purposes that are not on the list?

- to get to know other teachers
- to help develop a culture of cooperation in a school
- to share knowledge and experience with other teachers
- to solve problems
- to raise staff morale and motivation
- to reach decisions about important issues

2 Features of successful meetings: look at the list below and choose the three features that you think are the most important. Can you add to the list?

- Meetings should have a clear purpose.
- Meetings should be planned and structured.
- There should be an agenda and chairperson.
- Participants should be well prepared.
- Meetings should include appropriate participants.
- Meetings should include discussion and participation.
- Meetings should be managed in terms of time.
- There should be a follow-up action plan.

3 Meetings to support professional development are often of two kinds:

- Meetings to discuss or resolve problems. The goal of meetings of this kind is to examine a problem in depth and to identify strategies to address or resolve the problem. It should be a problem that requires group input. If there is a simple solution then there is no need for the meeting. Guidelines for meetings of this kind are:
    - Participants should be provided with relevant background information and examples before the meeting.
    - One person should manage the meeting and prepare an outline of the different stages in the meeting and the time allotted.
    - Participants should be those who are most affected by the problem as well as those with relevant experience and knowledge.
    - The group should brainstorm a variety of solutions and rank them according to how easy they would be to implement.
    - Then the group should identify the factors needed to implement the strategy and discuss any obstacles that might occur.
    - Next the group agrees on a solution that they will implement, review, and report back on.

- Meetings in which teachers report on conference or workshop participation. Teachers often have the opportunity to attend a workshop or conference and may be required to share what they learned with colleagues in the form of a meeting. Guidelines for these meetings are:
    - The presenter informs interested teachers in advance (by email or memo) of the nature of the conference and what its goals were.
    - Participants are informed of how the meeting will be structured.
    - The presenter prepares a handout about the seminar and includes summaries of the sessions that will be discussed.
    - If there was a theme for the conference or a particular topic the teacher focused on, the main issues that were discussed or main things that were learned should be the focus.
    - During the meeting, teachers should be encouraged to ask questions, and to discuss implications for follow-up.
    - Discussion should focus on the relevance of the conference to the needs of the school and the implications for practice.

43 Plan a workshop

Purpose: to learn how to plan an effective workshop

A workshop provides an excellent opportunity for an intensive, short-term learning activity based on a particular topic or set of skills. It enables a group of teachers to work together to master a new set of skills, to learn how to apply new teaching methods or materials, or to consider how to resolve an issue or problem they may have encountered in their teaching. In this tip we will review how to plan an effective workshop.

1 The nature of workshop: a workshop is a meeting or series of meetings in which a group of teachers take part in intensive discussion on a topic or activity of practical benefit to them or to their school. A focus on practical outcomes distinguishes a workshop from a meeting. Workshops allow you to learn from experts; they are intended to lead to practical application; they can support creativity and innovation; they also support the development of collegiality in a school.

2 Choosing a workshop topic: topics chosen for workshops should involve problem solving and the development of practical skills. The following are the kinds of topics that could be the focus of workshop:

- making the best use of technology
- using authentic materials to teach reading
- strategies for teaching mixed-level classes
- teaching young learners.

Topics such as these can be identified through surveying your teachers' needs and interests.

3 Timing: a workshop may take place over a morning, or if necessary, over one or more days depending on what it is intended to achieve.

4 Participants: choose a suitable number of participants. It is difficult to plan workshop activities for large numbers, since a successful workshop depends on the workshop leader interacting actively with the participants. If there are too many participants, the workshop may turn into a seminar. Thirty participants is probably the maximum number to

plan for, while workshops with as few as five can also be effective. Since workshops usually make use of group-based learning, group formation is important. Four or five participants in groups works well, and it is useful for one member to serve as group leader and reporter. He or she will provide the group's feedback.

5 Leading the workshop: a workshop is usually conducted by one or more specialists in a particular area or skill. Invite an expert or experienced practitioner to lead the workshop. Although the workshop will draw on the collective knowledge and skills of the group members, it is also important that the workshop leader is knowledgeable about the topic of the workshop and can give expert advice and opinions.

6 Structure the workshop: in order for participants to be able to learn new information, discuss and share ideas, and arrive at application to their own situations, a variety of activities can be used, including:

- Bonding activities – fun activities that enable participants to get to know each other and to feel comfortable with the group members.
- Direct teaching – the workshop leader presents key information.
- Tasks – activities in which participants plan, solve problems, and apply principles and procedures.
- Discussion – pair or group discussions.
- Breakaway groups – groups are set or choose different tasks, and work on them separately, then report back to the whole group.
- Practice activities – participants practice things they have learned.
- Demonstrations – members may present or demonstrate things they have completed in group sessions.
- Review and reflection – participants reflect on what they have learned from the workshop.

7 Follow up: obtain feedback from participants to get suggestions for future workshops using a feedback form or communication channels such as email listserves and social media groups. Follow through on distribution of summaries, handouts, products, and other items that may have been developed during the workshops. Contact participants at a later date to find out how they have been able to implement what they learned during the workshop.

Reinders, H. & Lewis, M. (2014). *Facilitating Workshops: A resource book for Lecturers and Trainers*. Palgrave MacMillan.

44 Start a suggestion box

> **Purpose: to use a suggestion box to share teaching ideas and to get feedback from students**

Over time we build up a rich source of knowledge about teaching, including how to respond to common situations and concerns. Using a suggestion box to share your knowledge with others can provide a useful resource for other teachers. A classroom suggestion box can also be a useful way of getting feedback and suggestions from students. This could be a physical box or an online suggestion box. For example, one of my student teachers found that one learner in her class often dominated lessons and spoke far more than the others. She asked students for suggestions for sharing talk among the class and received a number of good suggestions, including giving each student a set of three cards. They used each card whenever they asked a question or had something to say, and had to get the permission of their classmates if they wanted to go beyond their three questions. This tip describes the use of teacher and student suggestion boxes.

1 Teachers' suggestion box: the format of suggestion boxes traditionally consists of a physical box in which people place written suggestions or requests for suggestions from other teachers; however, technology provides a more convenient format such as a school website or wiki where you can post suggestions.

The suggestion box serves as a place where you can provide brief accounts of things you would like to share with other teachers. It also serves as a source of obtaining suggestions from colleagues. Examples of shared suggestions include:

- accounts of creative ways of using activities or resources
- great ideas
- reports on how students responded to an activity
- reports on how to solve a problem
- suggestions for useful resources
- tips on how to prepare students for tests.

The suggestion box is also a place where you can describe problems and get suggestions from your colleagues. For example:

- students talk too much in their native language during a lesson
- students take over control of the lesson
- one or two students dominate lessons
- students are unwilling to speak during a speaking activity
- students arrive late or disrupt the class
- students don't do their homework
- some students don't get on well together and don't want to work together.

2 Submitting or asking for a suggestion: briefly describe the class and course, who the students are, and provide any background information that may help understand the context.

- If you are sharing tips and suggestions, describe the situation where you used the idea or activity, how you used it, and why it was successful. Give any tips for others who might like to try it.
- If you are asking for suggestions from others, describe the problem you encountered, how you attempted to respond to it, and what effect it had. Add any other thoughts you may have about the issue and any surrounding factors that might help provide a better understanding of the issue.

3 Class suggestion box: the class box serves as a place where your students can place comments or suggestions relating to any aspect of a class. These can be brief notes rather than extended written suggestions. It provides a place where students can place both brief comments on things they liked, as well as suggestions for future lessons.

4 Clarify with the students the kinds of suggestions you would like them to contribute: these could include comments on aspects of a lesson they liked or found useful, things they think could be improved as well as things they would like to see included in future lessons. Students should feel free to make suggestions anonymously and to do so when they feel they have something they would like you to consider.

Review the suggestions regularly and use them to reflect on your teaching. If appropriate, you may sometimes want to discuss them with your students.

Share your knowledge and skills

A successful school consists of teachers who see themselves as a community with shared concerns and interests, and who can learn from each other's knowledge, skills, and experience.

45. Join an online discussion forum
46. Make a presentation
47. Write for a magazine or online publication
48. Become a mentor
49. Team-teach with a colleague
50. Learn through peer coaching

Join an online discussion forum

When we are not teaching, much of our time at school is spent in conversation with other teachers. Conversation is an important way of sharing expertise and discussing issues and problems, and I have strong memories of many conversations I have had with colleagues. These days, of course, the internet provides a virtual means that makes it possible to interact with other teachers in many different parts of the world and offers some great opportunities for professional development. This tip describes how to interact with other teachers through the means of an online discussion forum or ODF.

1 There are two main kinds of ODFs:

- *General purpose ODFs* are aimed at all teachers no matter what level or kind of course they teach.
- *Special-purpose forums* are for teachers with interests in a particular area, such as teaching ESP, teaching business English, or materials development.

A forum may also contain a number of sub-forums, each of which may have discussions of several topics. When a discussion starts on a particular topic it is called a thread, and other members of the forum can add their replies. With some forums, members need to register and then log in each time they add a comment, but most do not. A forum is different from a chatroom, where messages may not be permanently archived. A forum usually has an administrator and one or more moderators.

2 Benefits of ODFs: through joining an ODF you can interact with other teachers in your own time and place. You can also choose what and when to learn; share teaching resources, advice, and ideas; help resolve problems; upload or download materials, tests, and video activities. Discussion boards or threaded discussions allow for discussions to develop over a period of time and enable you to become part of a world-wide community of teachers with shared interests. Other benefits of ODFs include:

- They take place privately and without the embarrassment that face-to-face conversations might create if a teacher feels the need to discuss difficulties they are facing or anxieties that need to be resolved.
- They preserve a record of the conversations that can be reviewed and considered at a later date.

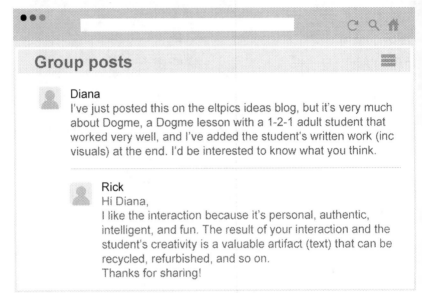

Group posts

Diana
I've just posted this on the eltpics ideas blog, but it's very much about Dogme, a Dogme lesson with a 1-2-1 adult student that worked very well, and I've added the student's written work (inc visuals) at the end. I'd be interested to know what you think.

Rick
Hi Diana,
I like the interaction because it's personal, authentic, intelligent, and fun. The result of your interaction and the student's creativity is a valuable artifact (text) that can be recycled, refurbished, and so on.
Thanks for sharing!

3 Factors that affect the benefits of an ODF: the success of an ODF will depend on a number of factors. These include:

- The purpose and focus of the forum. If it is too unfocussed, it may not be productive.
- It is important to establishing a supportive and trusting atmosphere among participants. Rules need to be established for appropriate styles of communication or "netiquette".
- Comments should be brief and relevant to the topic of the discussion. They should not become a forum for complaints.
- Interactions between members should work towards resolution of an issue or problem.
- Membership should include both experienced and novice teachers.
- The moderator should post a summary of the discussion.

Cullen, R., Kullman, J., & Wild, C. (2013). Online collaborative learning on an ESL teacher education program. *ELT Journal 67(4)*, 425–434.

Purpose: to clarify and share ideas through making a presentation

---

Sharing ideas with colleagues through presentations enables you to share innovative ideas and practices, clarify issues and problems, and it provides an opportunity to develop a sense of collegiality in a school. This tip focuses on how to use presentations within a teacher support group or at professional event such as a workshop or conference.

1 Presentations: I still remember clearly the first presentation I made. It was in Albuquerque, New Mexico. As a young scholar I guess I wanted to demonstrate that I knew something. The audience listened politely. Afterwards a respected professor gave me some useful advice: "Don't try to tell people everything you know!". Over the years, I have found myself giving presentations to groups as small as ten and as large as 2,000, and more often these days through webinars and other online sites. This has meant learning to improve my presentation skills.

2 Topics for presentations: a wide variety of topics are suitable for presentations. You could consider the following areas:

- a report on teacher research, such as an action research project
- a presentation of a set of materials and activities you have prepared
- a case study of a successful or unsuccessful learner or of a class that created a particular challenge for you
- a presentation based on a conference or professional seminar you have attended.

3 Guidelines for making presentations. Here is a list of suggestions I try to keep in mind when I plan and deliver presentations.

- Start with a strong opening to catch people's attention. It is hard to regain interest if you lose it at the beginning.
- Keep your introduction short and sweet. Get to the point. Tell the audience what you will focus on and what you hope they will get out of the talk.

- Keep your audience in mind. Why is this information worth sharing? What's in it for them? Make it relevant to your audience's needs and interests.
- Keep to the main points and don't over-run. Don't try to tell your audience everything you know. Be concise. Remember that even adults have limited attention spans.
- Prepare notes. But don't read from your notes.
- Make sure people can hear you, and don't talk too fast.
- Try using pitch and tone to make your voice more interesting and hold your audience's attention.
- Is there a story that you can use in your talk? Stories help your audience pay attention and remember things. If you can bring in a story or a personal experience, your audience is more likely to pay attention to you and to remember your points afterwards.
- If you use slides, don't read them aloud. Your audience can read them for themselves. Keep any graphics clear and simple. Your slides should contain less, rather than more, information. If you need to provide more information, you can prepare a handout. You might be familiar with the 10-20-30 rule for slideshows:
  - Use no more than 10 slides
  - Talk for no more than 20 minutes
  - Use a font size of no less than 30 point.

  So speak to the audience and not to your slides.

- Smile and connect with your audience through eye contact, and distribute your attention equally.
- Keep to the point. Don't skip around or use slides that don't tell a part of your story.
- Use gestures and movement. Don't stand like a robot, but move around.
- Check out the technology in advance, and have a back-up plan in case it doesn't work.
- If you plan to have a Q&A at the end of your presentation, have a few questions ready in case the audience is slow to come up with some.

Write for a magazine or online publication

Purpose: to learn how to publish an article about teaching

The field of language teaching makes progress through teachers, researchers, and other professionals sharing their knowledge and experience. One way this occurs is through the many different kinds of professional publications that are available in the field. This tip focuses on how to write an article for publication for an audience of teachers.

1 Types of publications: there are many different kinds of publications for teachers, which may be in print form, both in print and online, or only available online. These include:

- local or regional publications
- international journals such as *ELT Journal*
- publications for a special audience such as ESP practitioners, teachers of young learners, or teacher trainers.

Some publications primarily focus on practice, while others are geared either towards integrating research, theory and practice, or towards research and theory.

2 Purpose of writing for publication: all publications, no matter their audience, depend on contributions from teachers like you. And writing for a suitable publication is a good way not only of sharing ideas and experience with others, but also of clarifying your own ideas about an issue or topic. Increasingly, journals are now online and can publish more quickly than in the past. Writing content for websites for publishers or teaching organizations is also a great way to break into writing.

3 Decide on the kind of publication you feel you could write for: is it an online publication, a newsletter, a magazine, or research journal?

The next step is to familiarize yourself with your chosen publication, its audience, the content of the articles it publishes, and the style and level of articles it publishes. Who are typical contributors? Are the publishers looking for articles, book reviews, reviews of teaching materials? What guidelines do they give for contributors to the publication? How should submissions be written and formatted?

4 Reflect on your own teaching experience and situation: you might have an interesting or novel teaching idea, an experience that prompts rethinking, or additional ideas about a topic you might like to respond to and expand on. Can you add a new angle to a topic that has been written about lately? Can you share classroom research or other forms of inquiry related to your teaching?

5 Decide if you would like to work on your own or collaborate with another teacher: if you are new to writing, it is often easier to write with a colleague. If an article has two authors, their names are normally listed alphabetically on the published article, except when one author has taken a major role in the paper, in which case his or her name may appear first.

6 Brainstorm ideas for the article: what will the main focus of it be? How will you develop it? What kinds of information and examples will you be able to include? Be guided here by articles that are typically published in the magazine or forum you wish to contribute to.

7 Show a draft of what you have written to your colleagues: don't be discouraged by criticism or suggestions for rewriting. Even experienced writers often go through many different versions of articles they write. (This book, for example, went through several major rewrites based on the feedback from my ruthless editor – Scott Thornbury!)

8 When you think your article is ready for submission, send it to the journal editors and hope for the best. Your article may be sent out for review by other professionals selected by the journal editor, and it may take some time before you know whether your article has been accepted, whether it will be accepted subject to some revisions, or whether it is not considered suitable for the magazine.

In the case of rejection, do not be discouraged from trying again. Every person who writes for publication will confirm that the feedback you get, both positive and negative, is an essential part of the learning process.

Purpose: to understand the role of mentoring

One of the roles I have enjoyed in my career has been the role of mentor. Mentoring is the process by which an experienced teacher assists a novice teacher to develop his or her personal and professional skills. In this tip we examine the nature of mentoring and the role of a mentor-teacher.

1 Purpose: the goal of mentoring is for novice teachers to get feedback on their teaching. It involves giving structured individual guidance and support to someone who is fairly new to teaching.

2 Benefits of mentoring: mentoring has benefits for both the person you mentor as well as for you as mentor. For the novice teacher, mentoring can help:

- improve teaching skills
- make connections between coursework theory and practice
- strengthen a sense of professional identity
- provide opportunities to observe an experienced teacher.

For the mentor, mentoring can help:

- gain new perspectives on teaching
- encourage reflection on your own beliefs and practices
- provide opportunities to develop skills of observation and of providing feedback, guidance, and advice to novice teachers
- increase your job satisfaction and enthusiasm for teaching.

3 Mentoring procedures: a mentoring relationship may be a voluntary activity (such as when a new teacher asks to be mentored by an experienced teacher), or it may be a requirement of the institution.

Mentoring involves observation of both the mentor's and mentee's classes, regular meetings between you as mentor and your mentee to discuss the observations, and identification of strategies your mentee could implement. Other activities could involve team teaching, shared lesson planning, and observations.

4 Focus on specific aspects of teaching: mentoring seeks to improve teaching and is more effective if it has a specific focus. For example, mentoring would be useful if your mentee had concerns such as:

- how to address problems of classroom management
- how to make lessons more motivating
- how to make effective use of an assigned textbook
- how to make effective use of pair and group activities
- how to make effective use of technology.

5 Giving feedback: mentoring makes use of written accounts of the observations, conversations, and other activities that involve you and the novice teacher. This could take the form of a journal that your mentee keeps during the mentoring process. The journal could also include accounts of incidents or reflections for discussion with you.

6 Timing: the timing of the mentor–mentee experience will vary depending on the purpose of the mentoring as well as the logistics it involves. For example, a novice teacher may work with you as mentor for a semester or for the duration of a course.

7 Requirements for a mentor-teacher: the success of mentoring depends on the skill and knowledge you bring as mentor-teacher. Mentors need an advanced level of professional knowledge and teaching skills, and to know how to communicate this to novice teachers. The ability to provide feedback and emotional support for trainee teachers in a non-judgmental way are important mentoring skills.

8 Implementing mentoring: the following steps are involved in implementing a mentoring program:

- Find out who would be interested in serving as mentors.
- Provide opportunities to learn about the process of mentoring.
- Clarify how mentoring will be implemented.
- Offer mentoring opportunities to novice teachers.
- You and your mentee decide which aspects of teaching to focus on and how you will carry out your mentoring activities.

Bailey, K. (2006). *Language Teacher Supervision: A case-based approach*. Cambridge: Cambridge University Press.

Chick, M. (2015). The education of language teachers: instruction or conversation. *ELT Journal 69(3)*, 297–307.

Smith, M. K., & Lewis, M. (2015). Toward facilitative mentoring and catalytic interventions. *ELT Journal 69(2)*, 140–150.

Team-teach with a colleague 49

49

Purpose: to learn through sharing the teaching of a lesson

Have you ever shared a class with another teacher, in an activity known as team-teaching? If not, I recommend you try it. It can be fun, as well as a great learning opportunity for everyone involved. Team-teaching (also called co-teaching) refers to two teachers sharing the responsibility for planning and teaching a class. It involves a cycle of planning, teaching, and then sharing reflections on what was learned through the process. This tip explores the benefits of team-teaching and how it can be implemented.

1 Purpose: the goal of team-teaching is to enable you and a colleague to learn from collaboration, enabling you to compare teaching styles and to share expertise.

2 Benefits of team-teaching: team-teaching can offer different kinds of benefits and opportunities. These include:

- Teachers can observe different teaching styles.
- Learners can receive more individual attention.
- The school develops a culture of collegiality.

3 Planning for team-teaching: the choice of teaching partner is important in team-teaching since both of you should be comfortable working together. There are different kinds of participation in team-teaching. What do you think the benefits are for the two partners in these pairings?

- equal partners (both teachers have an equal amount of experience and knowledge)
- mentor and apprentice
- native-speaker teacher and non-native-speaker teacher

Some benefits include:

- Equal partners compare different ways of presenting lessons.
- The mentor acquires mentoring skills: the apprentice observes how an expert deals with problems.

- The native-speaker teacher observes how the non-native-speaker teacher uses the first language to facilitate learning.
- The non-native-speaker teacher can compare their language use with that of the native-speaker teacher.

4 Planning the team-teaching lesson: team-teaching involves collaboration at each stage of the lesson. Before the lesson, you and your colleague develop a plan for the lesson which maps out the activities that your lesson will include and the time needed for each activity.

At this stage, a decision is needed on how the lesson will be divided between you. There are several options:

- Both of you share each stage of the lesson, such as the lesson opening, the teaching activities, and the closing.
- Divide the activities between you. One of you handles the opening, then you take turns teaching the different activities in the lesson.
- Divide the teaching according to skills. For example, one of you handles speaking and grammar, the other listening and reading.
- One of you complements the other, for example, by providing examples or writing on the board while the other is presenting.

5 During the lesson: when one of you is handling your part of the lesson, it is important to clarify the role of the other. For example, your co-teacher could:

- move around the class and monitor students' performance
- assist students who need extra support or guidance for activities
- sit at the back of the class and observe the students' participation
- participate in the lesson as a student, while being careful not to take over the role of the students.

6 After the lesson: review together your experience of the lesson, what worked well, what could have worked better, and reflect on what you learned from team-teaching. You should also consider what benefits you felt you obtained from the experience, and how you think it benefited your learners. You may then decide on future team-taught lessons.

Ng, M. L. (2005). Difficulties with team-teaching in Hong Kong kindergartens. *ELT Journal* 69(2), 188–197.

Learn through peer coaching

50

Purpose: to help a teacher acquire new teaching skills

Peer coaching is a great way of learning from a colleague. We often forget how much some of our colleagues know. Peer coaching is a painless way of tapping into other teachers' expertise, and involves working with another teacher to develop or improve some aspect of your teaching. It is different from mentoring, where the mentee is a novice teacher (see Tip 48): in peer coaching both teachers may be equally experienced but with different skill sets. And it has benefits for both teachers. The "coach" can be a source of new teaching ideas and techniques. "Wow, I have never tried to use a text in that way. It's really effective!" Serving as a coach is also a sign of professional recognition and provides an opportunity for you to reflect on and clarify your own approach to teaching. And, of course, peer coaching can also help develop a sense of collegiality in a school.

In this tip we will review the nature of peer coaching and how you might implement it.

1 Situations for peer coaching: there are two common situations when peer coaching is useful. These are:

- when a teacher takes on an unfamiliar teaching assignment and seeks to benefit from the knowledge and skill of an experienced teacher, such as when a senior teacher wants to teach a class of teenagers for the first time.
- when a teacher is experiencing a difficulty with some aspect of a new teaching assignment and needs advice or support from a colleague.

2 Stages in the peer coaching process: if you wish to be coached:

- Indicate a wish to engage in peer coaching and describe the area you would like to focus on.
- You are linked to someone who has experience in that area.
- You meet and discuss the focus of the coaching experience. The coach may suggest books or articles to read, or refer you to online sources.
- The coach invites you to observe one or more of their classes to see how they handle the issue. The coach also observes your class.

- Following the observations, you meet for an informal conversation during which you discuss what you observed in each other's class, what issues arose, and what suggestions the coach can offer. The kind of feedback the coach offers during this process should generally be non-judgemental, and it should lead to specific strategies or suggestions for you to implement in subsequent lessons.
- You implement the coaches suggestions and have subsequent follow-up observations and conversations until the issue has been resolved.

3 Other ways in which peer coaching can be used: you can implement peer coaching in other ways, including the suggestions below.

- Shared materials development activities. If you have experience in developing materials (e.g. for an ESP class), work with another teacher on the development of teaching resources.
- Peer observation. You and a colleague take turns observing each other's classes in order to compare how you address specific aspects of teaching, such as error correction or the use of group work.
- Team-teaching. You and a colleague occasionally share a class, with each of you taking responsibility for different parts of the lesson (see Tip 49). Following the lesson, review what happened and compare your teaching approaches.
- Video-watching. You may video one or more of your lessons and review the video with your coach.

4 Implementing peer coaching: the following steps are useful in implanting a program of peer coaching in your school.

- Find out what your colleagues think about the benefits of peer coaching.
- Invite interested teachers to serve as coaches.
- Develop a plan as to how coaching activities would take place, including how often, when, and with which participants.
- Invite teachers to participate on a voluntary basis, and have them form pairs in which an experienced teacher works with a less-experienced colleague.
- Have the teachers decide which aspects of teaching to focus on and how they would conduct their observations and coaching experiences.

Stillwell, C. (2009). The collaborative development of teacher training skills. *ELT Journal*, *63(4)*, 353–362.

Appendix 1

Tip 4 Lesson report form for a grammar lesson

1. The main focus in the lesson was:
   a. Mechanics (e.g. punctuation and capitalization) ☐
   b. Rules of grammar (e.g. subject-verb agreement) ☐
   c. Communicative grammar practice ☐

2. The amount of time spent on grammar work was:
   a. The whole class period ☐
   b. Most of the class ☐
   c. About .... minutes ☐

3. I decided what grammar to teach based on:
   a. The textbook ☐
   b. The course syllabus ☐
   c. Students' performance on a test ☐
   d. Students' errors in oral and written work ☐
   e. Other .... ☐

4. I taught grammar by:
   a. Explaining grammar rules ☐
   b. Using visual aids ☐
   c. Discussing students' errors ☐
   d. Assigning exercises from the textbook ☐
   e. Giving exercises I designed ☐
   f. Other .... ☐

5. When assigning student work on grammar I had students:
   a. Study rules of grammar ☐
   b. Practice exercises orally in class ☐
   c. Practice exercises on the computer ☐
   d. Do exercises for homework ☐
   e. Do exercises based on errors in their written work ☐
   f. Keep a record of their errors ☐
   g. Go over each other's classwork or homework ☐
   h. Do sentence combining ☐
   i. Create sentences and paragraphs using grammar rules ☐
   m. Other .... ☐

Appendix 2

Tip 9. Review designs for lesson plans: Sample lesson plan template

Type of lesson: ....

Course: ....

Class: ....

Level of students: ....

Duration of lesson: ....

Lesson objectives: ....

Learning outcomes: ....

Materials used: ....

Groupings: ....

Anticipated problems: ....

LESSON PROCEDURES:	What the teacher will do	What the learner will do

1 OPENING:

a) Links to previous learning.

Time:

Steps:

1	1...	1...
	....	....
2	2...	2...
	....	....

etc.

b) Lead in to the main activity to create interest in the lesson.

Time:

Steps:

1	1...	1...
	....	....
2	2...	2...
	....	....

2 INSTRUCTION:

The main activities of the lesson.

Time:

Steps:

1	1.	1. ....
	....	....
2	2.	2. ....
	....	....

3 CLOSURE:

Review and preview of future learning.

Time:

Steps:

1	1.	1. ....
	....	....
2	2.	2. ....
	....	....

etc.

4 FOLLOW UP:

Assign independent work or homework.

Time:

Steps:

1	1.	1. ....
	....	....
2	2.	2. ....
	....	....

etc

5 SELF EVALUATION AND COMMENTS AFTER THE LESSON:

....

Appendix 3

Tip 11 Develop a lesson observation form

Lesson observation form

Name of teacher:		Class:	
Name of observer:		Branch:	
Date:		Number of students:	

To the observer: for each of the criteria below, check the appropriate column.

F- Fully; M- Most of the time; P- Partially; NA- Non applicable

A	Planning – Evidence of effective lesson planning and preparation	F	M	P	No	NA
	1. The lesson was logically sequenced.					
	2. The activities were suitable for the age, level and needs of the group.					
	3. The activities were directly related to the aims and objectives of the lesson.					
	4. The class contained a variety of activities appropriate for the different learning styles (visual-receptive, audio-receptive, and motor-receptive).					
	5. Practice in different language skills was provided.					
	6. The teacher designed student-centred activities.					

B	Instructing – Effective language and lesson objective scaffolding	F	M	P	No	NA
	1. The teacher made the aims and objectives of the lesson clear to the learner and provided linguistic scaffolding.					
	2. The lesson was well paced.					
	3. Instructions and explanations were brief and clear.					
	4. The textbook and materials were effectively integrated into the class (realia, flashcards, games and a variety of media skills, such as Internet access, audiovisual aids, broadcast communications, etc).					
	5. The teacher was able to adjust instruction when the lesson was not working.					

Instructing – Effective language and lesson objective scaffolding	F	M	P	No	NA
6. The teacher used resources and strategies that build on learners' reasoning, problem solving and critical thinking skills, helping them become independent learners.					
7. The board was effectively used as a teaching tool.					

C	Learning	F	M	P	No	NA
	1. Genuine communicative interaction took place.					
	2. The teacher encouraged the students to use the target language all the time. / The teacher spoke in the target language all the time.					
	3. Student participation was encouraged through questions, examples, definitions, explanations, comments and peer correction.					
	4. Student talk was maximized and teacher's was minimized, when possible.					
	5. The teacher fostered collaborative learning by means of effective pair-work / group-work activities.					

D	Assessing	F	M	P	No	NA
	1. Students' errors were monitored and corrected effectively.					
	2. Student performance was effectively monitored, throughout the class, to check if the lesson objectives were being reached.					

E	Interpersonal Dynamics – Supportive environment that engages all learners	F	M	P	No	NA
	1. The teacher demonstrated awareness of individual students' needs.					
	2. The teacher made a conscious effort to pay attention to all students equally.					
	3. The teacher praised and encouraged the students.					
	4. The teacher used gestures, body language and/or humour to enliven the class.					
	5. The teacher modelled and promoted respectful, caring interactions which helped maintain a classroom atmosphere that was conducive to learning.					
	6. The seating arrangement was appropriate for each activity and allowed accessibility to the teacher.					
	7. The teacher made an effort to keep students attentive, engaged and interested throughout the class.					

F	Language, content, culture and digital literacy	F	M	P	No	NA
	1. The teacher spoke clearly and loudly enough for all to hear. / The teacher adjusted his/her speech to the English-language level of the learner.					
	2. The teacher used correct English grammar and pronunciation.					
	3. The teacher developed the student's awareness of the L2 culture. / The teacher maintained/modelled an impartial attitude towards cultural differences and/or conflicts.					
	4. The teacher was able to use the technological resources available in the classroom, coherently integrating them to enhance learning through the careful design and management of the activities and tasks to meet curricular goals and objectives.					

G	Attentiveness to institutional regulations	F	M	P	No	NA
	1. The class started / ended on time.					
	2. The teacher adopted an exemplary posture in class (e.g. dress code, physical decorum, etc.).					
	3. Teacher enforced institutional regulations and expectations regarding students' attitudes (e.g. gum chewing, slouching, using the cell phone, etc.).					

H	The Learners – Learners' performance and attitude in class	F	M	P	No	NA
	1. The learners were motivated and participated in all activities.					
	2. The learners used the target language among themselves and with the teacher.					
	3. The learners related very well with the group and the teacher.					
	4. The learners consistently used relatively correct English and demonstrated ability in self-correction.					

I	Commitment to Professionalism: Pre- and Post-conferences – Engagement in the observation process	F	M	P	No
	1. During the pre-observation conference, the teacher was able to clearly describe the lesson objectives and establish expectations for student behavior.				
	2. During the post-observation conference, the teacher demonstrated ability to reflect on his/her teaching practice and awareness of how stated objectives were accomplished.				

Index

Thanks

I am grateful to Karen Momber of Cambridge University Press for inviting me to contribute to the Tips series and for getting me started on this project. Scott Thornbury was a model series editor and provided extensive suggestions and guidance as I wrote, while my editor Alison Sharpe helped me polish and clarify my writing to make sure it said what I intended. I am also grateful to the teachers I have worked with over the years in many parts of the world and who have often tried out my suggestions as well as shared their tips for professional development with me.

Professor Jack C. Richards

Printed in the United States
By Bookmasters